Eyewitness
Shell

Silver cross inlaid with abalone shell

Green abalone

Oyster shell with mussel

Freshwater bivalve

Juvenile pen shell

Victor Dan's delphinula shell

Jamaican land snails

Fossil ammonite

Claw of European edible crab

Polygrati land snail she

Angular crab

Community of mollusk worm tubes

Cuban land snails

Lamellose wentletraps

Precious wentletrap

Eyewitness
Shell

Written by
ALEX ARTHUR

Japanese
wonder shell

Venus
comb murex

Cidaris
sea urchin

Slate pencil
sea urchin

Baby hawksbill turtle

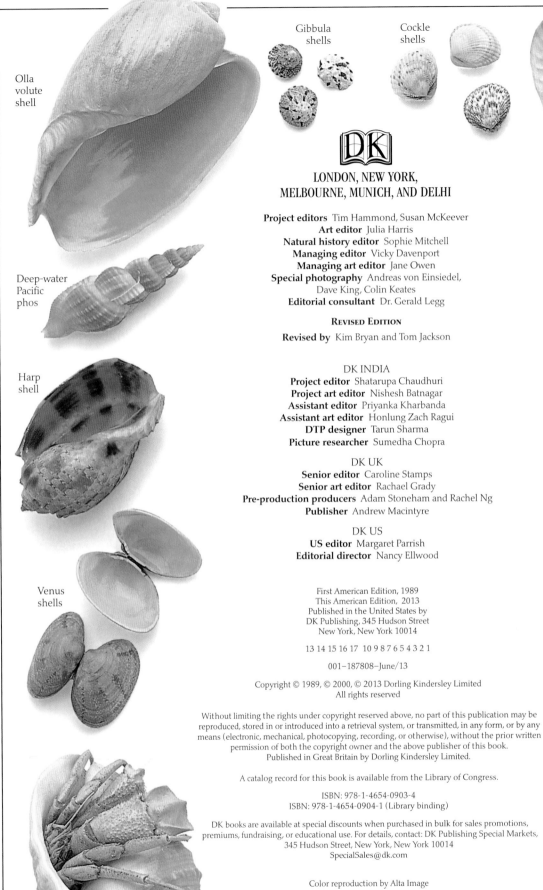

Olla
volute
shell

Gibbula
shells

Cockle
shells

DK

LONDON, NEW YORK, MELBOURNE, MUNICH, AND DELHI

Project editors Tim Hammond, Susan McKeever
Art editor Julia Harris
Natural history editor Sophie Mitchell
Managing editor Vicky Davenport
Managing art editor Jane Owen
Special photography Andreas von Einsiedel,
Dave King, Colin Keates
Editorial consultant Dr. Gerald Legg

REVISED EDITION

Revised by Kim Bryan and Tom Jackson

DK INDIA
Project editor Shatarupa Chaudhuri
Project art editor Nishesh Batnagar
Assistant editor Priyanka Kharbanda
Assistant art editor Honlung Zach Ragui
DTP designer Tarun Sharma
Picture researcher Sumedha Chopra

DK UK
Senior editor Caroline Stamps
Senior art editor Rachael Grady
Pre-production producers Adam Stoneham and Rachel Ng
Publisher Andrew Macintyre

DK US
US editor Margaret Parrish
Editorial director Nancy Ellwood

First American Edition, 1989
This American Edition, 2013
Published in the United States by
DK Publishing, 345 Hudson Street
New York, New York 10014

13 14 15 16 17 10 9 8 7 6 5 4 3 2 1

001–187808–June/13

A catalog record for this book is available from the Library of Congress.

ISBN: 978-1-4654-0903-4
ISBN: 978-1-4654-0904-1 (Library binding)

DK books are available at special discounts when purchased in bulk for sales promotions,
premiums, fundraising, or educational use. For details, contact: DK Publishing Special Markets,
345 Hudson Street, New York, New York 10014
SpecialSales@dk.com

Color reproduction by Alta Image
Printed in China by South China Printing Company

Deep-water
Pacific
phos

Harp
shell

Venus
shells

Scotch
bonnet

Hermit crab
in spiny
bonnet shell

Discover more at
www.dk.com

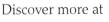

Dublin Bay
shrimp

Blunted
demoulia
shells

Contents

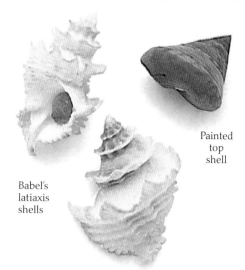

Babel's
latiaxis
shells

Painted
top
shell

What is a shell?

When we think of a shell, we usually picture the pretty specimens that can be collected from the beach during a seaside stroll. In fact, "shell" can describe many different things. The word *shell* actually means a hard outer casing that encloses and protects a variety of things, from fruit to baby birds, from snails to scurrying crabs. A shell, sometimes no more than a hardened skin, sometimes a thick and heavy mollusk shell, is always a means of protection—against predators and mechanical damage, or against extreme temperatures. Egg shells protect the unborn; nut shells enclose fruit and protect the seeds that give rise to new life. Many insects are protected by a hardened and segmented outer skin, and heavily thickened shells are found in crabs and lobsters. In living creatures, such as lobsters, the shell is called an exoskeleton, or external skeleton. One drawback of an exoskeleton is that it does not grow as the creature does, so the old shell must be shed and replaced by a new one big enough to accommodate the animal's larger size.

Hairs on husk

WORM SHELLS
Even worms can make shells. This colony (left), found at the bottom of an estuary (inlet), contains hundreds of hard, coiling tubes. Each one was once the home of a tiny marine worm.

HAIRY NUT
The fruit of the tropical coconut palm (right) can be bought in most parts of the world to eat. A thick, hard, hairy shell, or husk, encases the sweet, milky juices and white flesh. A soft skin covers the coconut when growing; it is usually removed before selling.

White flesh of nut

Shell

Seed

LUCKY BEANS
Sea beans, or "lucky" beans, grow in pods, mainly along the banks of the Amazon River in South America. The pods burst and drop their beans into the river. The beans are carried to the ocean and are polished by the saltwater. They are often used as lucky charms.

Ostrich shell

ARMORED ARMADILLO
The armadillo is one of the last remaining types of a group of armor-plated animals that flourished on Earth over 50 million years ago.

EGG SHELLS
Many creatures lay eggs in which their young can develop outside of the mother's body. The best known are those laid by birds; fertilized eggs hatch into fledglings, such as the baby pheasant above.

Pheasant hatching

...IG BIRD
...t 20 times the ...ze of a chicken's egg, ...he ostrich egg is one ...f the largest eggs ever ...roduced by a bird.

...KULL OR SHELL?
...Unlike shells, skeletons are internal, and ...nclosed by skin and flesh. You can, however, ...hink of a skull as a type of shell, since it encloses ...nd protects some soft organs, mainly the brain, ...while at the same time providing a framework to ...upport flesh and skin tissue. Mammals, birds, ...nd reptiles all have internal skeletons, each ...ne giving a creature its special shape.

Badger skull

Pincer

Segmented body

Sting

Four pairs of walking legs

SCORPION CASE
Like insects, scorpions are invertebrates (lacking a backbone) with a hardened outer casing that protects them. They belong to a group called spiders. Arachnids have long been thought to be closely related to insects and crustaceans (p. 22). Like crabs and lobsters, segmented and armored arachnids must shed their hardened casing in order to grow.

Creatures with shells

Of all the many different types of animal, only a few have a hard outer casing, or shell, to protect the internal organs of their body. Mammals, birds, reptiles, and fish have developed an internal skeleton for this purpose. Tortoises, turtles, and terrapins are the only vertebrate (backboned) animals that have both an internal skeleton and an external shell. Most of the other shelled creatures are invertebrates, which means they have no backbone, and many are very simple animals that have remained virtually unchanged for millions of years. Not all shells are the same: seashells and snail shells are made from layers of calcium carbonate, crab shells are formed from a substance called chitin, while tortoiseshell is made from plates of bone covered by keratin—a protein found in human fingernails.

Nautilus

LIVING DANGEROUSLY
A tentacled head extends from the shell of the living nautilus. Unlike many other mollusks, the creature is not fully enclosed by its shell, and therefore cannot hide when danger threatens.

Nautilus shell

Mollusks

The largest group of shelled creatures are the mollusks, of which there are more than 75,000 species, including snails, oysters, and squids. These versatile animals have evolved to live in the sea, in freshwater, and on land. Most mollusks have some kind of protective shell.

Edible land snails

SHELLED CEPHALOPOD
This shell belongs to the nautilus—a member of the most advanced group of mollusk: the cephalopods (p. 19). The nautilus is the only kind of cephalopod that still has a true external shell.

EDIBLE SNAIL
One of the best-known shells is that of the edible land snail. These creatures are now quite rare in the wild but are commercially farmed and sold as a gourmet food.

Portuguese oyster

INTERNAL SHELLS
Some mollusks have developed shells that are not visible from the outside. These spirula shells belong to a squidlike mollusk.

Spirula shells

JEWEL IN THE SHELL
Pearls are formed inside oysters (p. 36). These mollusks are known as bivalves—they have shells in two halves that are joined by an elastic ligament and held together by strong muscles. Edible oysters are farmed commercially like edible land snails (above).

Venus comb murex

SPINY SNAIL SHELL
Like the edible snail, this murex (spiny shell) belongs to a group of single-shelled mollusk known as gastropods (p. 12). This type of snail lives in the sea, where the variety of mollusks is greatest.

Reptiles

The reptiles belong to a varied group of cold-blooded vertebrate animals that includes snakes and lizards. Only turtles, tortoises, and terrapins (p. 28) have shells, and these are really only extensions of their internal skeletons.

TORTOISE SHELL
The bony shell of the tortoise makes a protective armor into which the animal can pull its head and legs in times of danger.

Moorish tortoise shell

SEA URCHIN TEST
The shell of a sea urchin is known as a test, and is made up of closely fitting plates that enclose the creature's soft parts.

Tropical sea urchin

Echinoderms

This group of primitive sea-dwelling creature includes starfish and sea cucumbers, which do not have shells, as well as sea urchins and sea potatoes (p. 20).

Florida sand dollar

Purple sea urchin

A SPINY SKIN
The tests of living sea urchins are covered with hundreds of spines that help the creature to move around on the seabed. Sometimes these spines are very sharp.

SAND DOLLARS
These flattened sea urchins have very tiny spines and are adapted for life on sandy shores (p. 21).

Crustaceans

There are more than 70,000 species of crustacean, including lobsters, shrimp, crabs, and barnacles. Most crustaceans have some sort of jointed shell, or carapace, and live in the oceans, although some have adapted to life in freshwater and on land.

Brown crab

BROWN HAIRY CRAB
This small crab lives in shallow-water rock pools, but relatives with leg spans of over 12 ft (3.5 m) can be found in deeper waters.

Atlantic barnacles

EDIBLE CRAB
In many parts of the world crab meat is considered a delicacy, and crabs are fished in large numbers using baited traps. The main shell of the crab protects the internal organs; the limbs are also covered in a hard, shell-like substance.

BARNACLES
Although they don't look much like crabs or lobsters, barnacles are also crustaceans. All barnacles are marine creatures and spend their lives attached to a hard base such as another shell or the hull of a boat. Barnacle shells are strengthened with plates made from calcium.

Living in a whorl

SHELL INSPIRED ART
The beautiful forms of seashells have influenced and inspired countless artists and architects throughout the centuries. Here, the radiating shape of a clam shell has been used to decorate an arched recess.

Despite the great variety in pattern, size, and weight, all seashells are made by the animals that live inside them, and all grow steadily outward. The whorl-shaped structures formed by the gastropod mollusks represent some of the most remarkable designs to be found anywhere in the natural world. Starting life as a tiny larva, the mollusk sets about building its shell by depositing calcium from the mantle—a fleshy fold on the animal's body. As the creature grows, the shell is extended outward in the form of a perfect spiral. Each type of seashell has a slightly different design, and this unique shape is passed on to each new generation.

Buoyancy chambers

Cross-section of nautilus shell

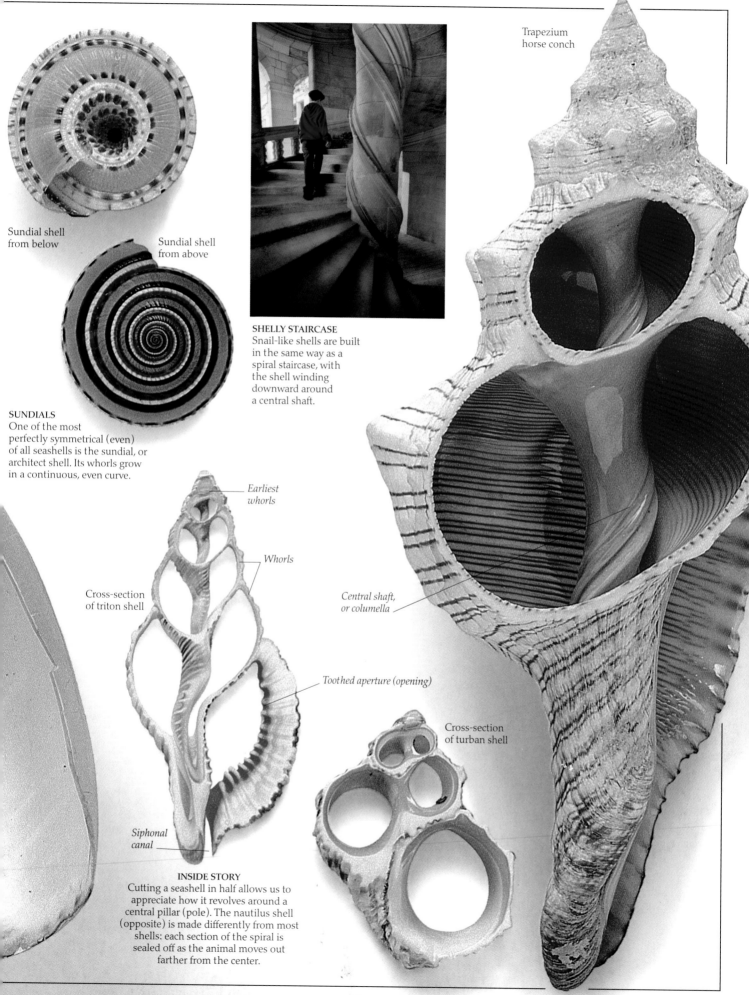

Trapezium horse conch

Sundial shell from below

Sundial shell from above

SHELLY STAIRCASE
Snail-like shells are built in the same way as a spiral staircase, with the shell winding downward around a central shaft.

SUNDIALS
One of the most perfectly symmetrical (even) of all seashells is the sundial, or architect shell. Its whorls grow in a continuous, even curve.

Earliest whorls

Whorls

Cross-section of triton shell

Toothed aperture (opening)

Central shaft, or columella

Cross-section of turban shell

Siphonal canal

INSIDE STORY
Cutting a seashell in half allows us to appreciate how it revolves around a central pillar (pole). The nautilus shell (opposite) is made differently from most shells: each section of the spiral is sealed off as the animal moves out farther from the center.

11

Snails of the world

Doris harp shell

IF YOU PICK UP A SEASHELL from the beach, chances are you will have found the empty shell of a sea snail. Snails belong to a large group of mollusks otherwise known as gastropods, or univalve shells. Both these names describe certain distinctive features: the word *gastropod* is derived from the Greek words for "stomach" and "foot" and, in simple terms, it is around the massive foot of a snail that all its important organs are based. The term *univalve* describes the single shell, often coiled in a spiral shape, that many gastropods inhabit—as opposed to the two-piece shells that are a feature of the bivalves (p. 16). The gastropods are the largest group of mollusks, and there are more than 50,000 different types living in the world's seas.

Bengal fig shell

FRAGILE FIGS
The graceful and extremely fragile fig shell lives in warm waters. When alive, it covers much of the shell with its body.

TROPICAL HARP SHELLS
The beautiful harp shell gets its name from the smooth ribs spaced regularly around the shell, which resemble the strings of a harp.

THE COLOR PURPLE
Purple dye can be made from some mollusks, including certain types of murex (spiny shells). The ancient Phoenicians were the first to discover this art, and their Tyrian purple cloth—named after the city of Tyre where it was made—was worn by Roman nobles as a symbol of their wealth. Purple has been regarded as a royal color ever since, and the ceremonial robes of many kings and queens are still made of purple cloth to this day.

WARM-WATER FROGS
So called because of their roughly textured appearance, frog shells can be found in most warm seas. Large specimens were once used to make oil lamps.

Geography cone

DEADLY POISON CONES
Cone shells live in most seas and feed mainly on small fish and worms. They are among the most sought after of all shells, and are well known for their ability to paralyze their prey with a tiny, barbed and poisonous "harpoon." One of the most highly poisonous cone shells is the geography cone from the Indo-Pacific (Asian Pacific to Indian Ocean). It has been responsible for a number of human deaths. Any cone shell you find should be handled very carefully.

Noble frog shell

Common distorsio

DISTORTED DISTORSIOS
Found mainly in tropical seas, the distorsio shell has a strangely inflated and distorted appearance. These shells are members of the Personidae family and are also closely related to frog shells (above left).

REAL CONCHES
Many types of seashell are commonly referred to as conch shells, but the name really only applies to a family of about 60–75 widely distributed shells. The best known is the large pink conch from the West Indies, a shell that is often used as food and as an ornament. Semi-precious pink pearls have been found inside some shells.

Roman nobleman with Tyrian purple cape

Trunculus murex

Rose-branch murex

Purple-dye murex shells

SPINY BEAUTIES
There are many different types of murex shells. They are usually decorated with attractive frills and spines.

Bubonian conch

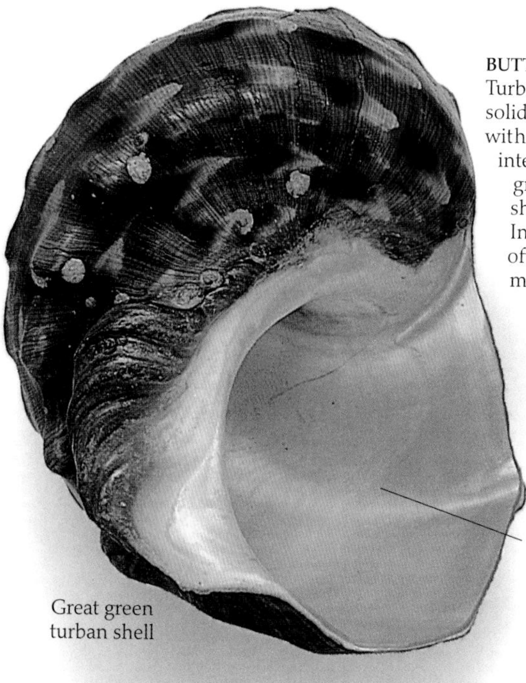

BUTTON UP
Turban shells are solid, heavy shells with mother-of-pearl interiors. The great green turban shell of the Indo-Pacific is often used to make buttons.

Festive volute

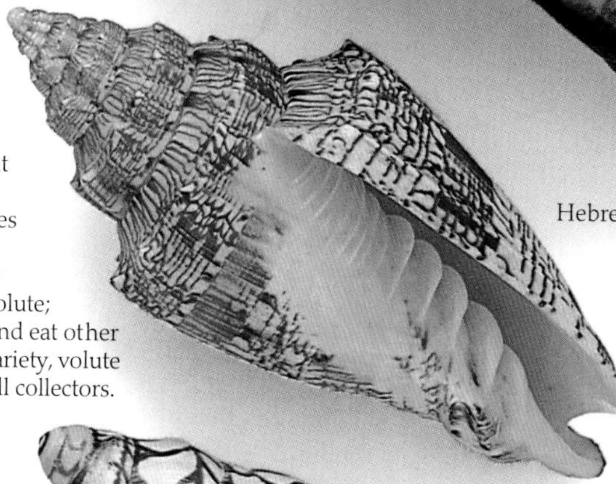

Mother-of-pearl interior

Great green turban shell

VALUABLE VOLUTES
These large and often brightly patterned shells occur in most seas, but the largest number of species is found off Australian coasts. Cold-water volutes are not as colorful as the warm-water types shown here. There are more than 200 species of volute; most of these live in sand and eat other animals. Because of their variety, volute shells are popular with shell collectors.

Hebrew volute

HAIRY TRUMPET SHELLS
The best known of the triton shells is triton's trumpet (p. 32), which is blown as a horn in various parts of the world. Some tritons are brightly colored but, when alive, they are usually covered with a fibrous hair that makes the shell difficult to see (p. 41).

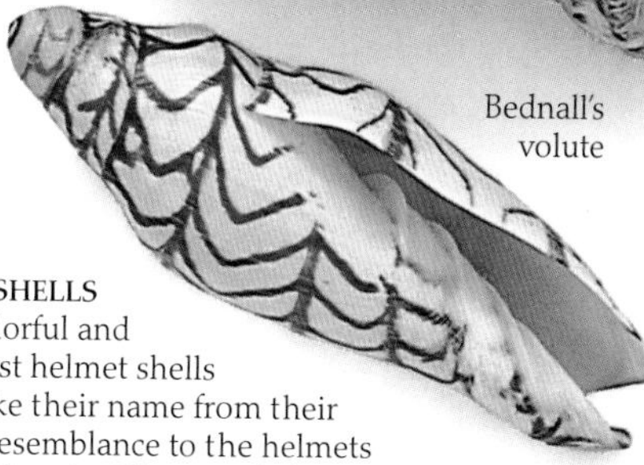

Black-spotted triton

Bednall's volute

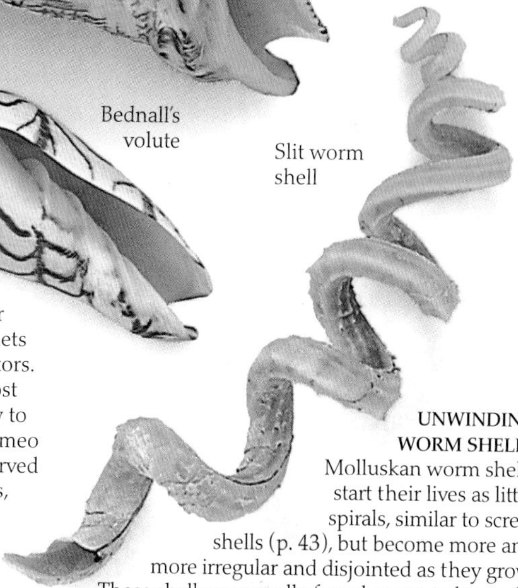

Slit worm shell

CAMEO SHELLS
The colorful and robust helmet shells take their name from their resemblance to the helmets of ancient Roman gladiators. They can be found in most warm seas and some grow to 12 in (30 cm) in length. Cameo brooches are traditionally carved from bullmouth helmet shells, which are mainly found off the coast of East Africa.

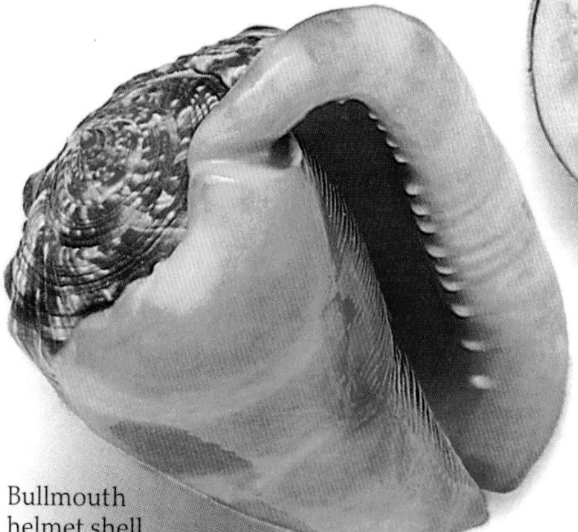

Victorian cameo

UNWINDING WORM SHELLS
Molluskan worm shells start their lives as little spirals, similar to screw shells (p. 43), but become more and more irregular and disjointed as they grow. These shells are usually found cemented to rocks or buried in sponges and sand because their uncoiled shells are not suited to mobility.

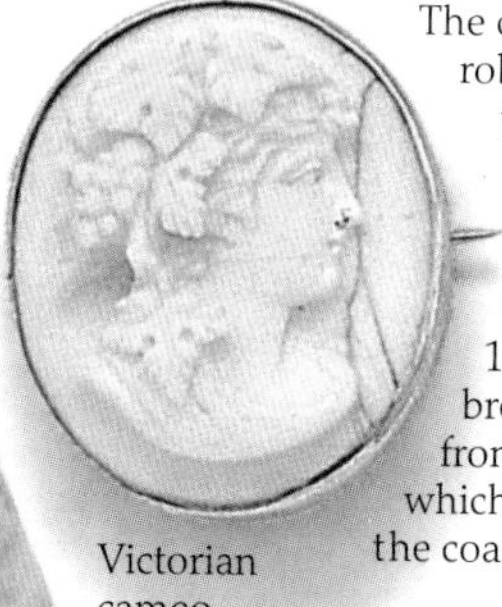

SHINY EGGS
The egg shells, such as the shuttlecock volva, are closely related to the true cowries, but are seldom as colorful.

Bullmouth helmet shell

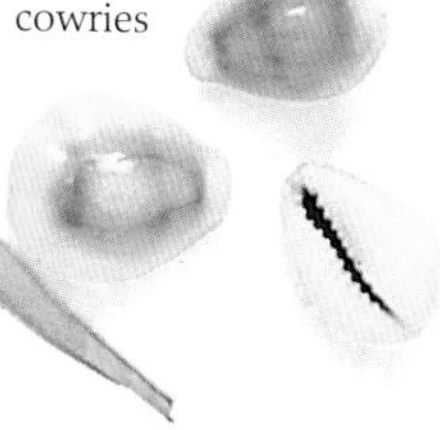

Money cowries

"JEWELS OF THE DEPTHS"
Cowries are among the best known of all gastropod mollusks; their glossy, chinalike shells look almost as if they have been varnished but are actually quite natural. Cowries have always been valued for their beauty, and their bright colors make them popular with modern shell collectors—some of the rarer types have been known to sell for more than $20,000! Most of the 200 or so types of cowrie live in tropical areas, often close to coral reefs.

Cylindrical cowrie

Cowrie helmet

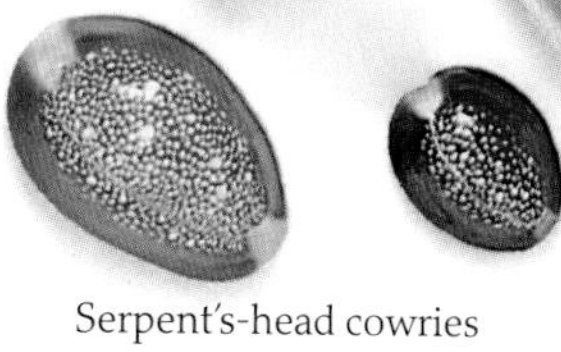

Serpent's-head cowries

Shuttlecock volva

Continued on next page

Australian
pheasant shell

Precious
wentletrap

Royal paper
bubble shell

White-banded
bubble shell

European
china limpets

Humphrey's
whelk

STAIRCASE FORGERY
The wentletrap is one
of the most distinctive
of all seashells. Its name is
derived from the German word
Wendeltreppe, meaning "spiral staircase." This
shell was once so rare that Chinese merchants are
said to have sold forgeries made out of rice paste.

BREAKABLE BUBBLES
So called because of their
fragile, inflated appearance,
these paper-thin shells offer
little protection to the mollusks,
which are often much larger
than the shells they carry.

LUSTROUS LIMPETS
Limpets are some of the
best-known mollusks,
being commonly found on coastal
rocks, attached securely by their strong
feet. Some types have a hole at the top
of the shell and are known as keyhole
limpets. The inside of a limpet shell often
has an iridescent (rainbowlike) shine.

White-zoned
goblet shell

Black-mouthed
goblet shell

Pimpled
dog whelk

WHELKS OF THE WORLD
Found in great numbers in
most of the world's seas—
including both polar
and tropical waters—
the whelks are a very
large family of marine
mollusk and are
fished commercially in
many parts of the world.

Ridged
goblet shell

Glans
dog whelk

Clathrate
dog whelk

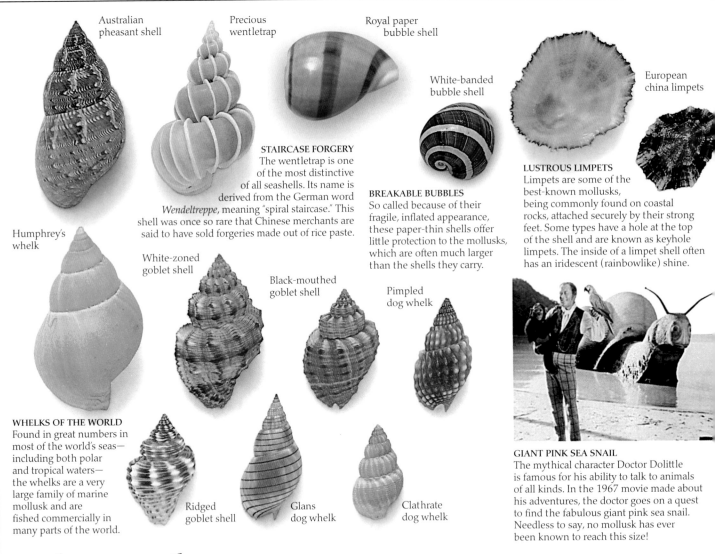

GIANT PINK SEA SNAIL
The mythical character Doctor Dolittle
is famous for his ability to talk to animals
of all kinds. In the 1967 movie made about
his adventures, the doctor goes on a quest
to find the fabulous giant pink sea snail.
Needless to say, no mollusk has ever
been known to reach this size!

Freshwater snails

Most types of snail live in the ocean, but many gastropods
can also be found living in freshwater habitats. Some
types absorb air from the water through gills; others have
lungs and have to come to the surface to breathe. The
patterns and colors of freshwater shells tend to be less
vivid compared to those of marine species. Freshwater
snails can be found living on weeds and rushes or in
mud and sand; empty shells are often cast up on
riverbanks, especially after flooding.

GIANT AFRICAN RIVER SNAIL
One of the largest freshwater snails occurs in the rivers
of southeast Africa. Although it reaches a length of more
than 5 in (12 cm), the shell of the giant African river snail
is amazingly lightweight and fragile. In the ocean, a shell of
this size would normally be crusted
with all kinds of growths, but in
freshwater, shells usually have
only a coat of algae that
is easily removed.

OUT OF AFRICA
The strange-looking tiphorbia
snail is just one of the hundreds of
unique snail shells found in Lake
Tanganyika in Africa. This huge
expanse of landlocked
water has developed a
range of mollusks that
are more like marine than
freshwater gastropods.

GREAT POND SNAIL
This fragile snail is extremely
common in lakes and ponds
all over Europe. When
alive, the shell has a
greenish color;
actually it is
semitransparent,
and the green is
the color of the
mollusk inside.

Tiphorbia
snail

RAM'S-HORN SHELL
The flattened spiral shape
of the ram's-horn snail
is fairly common.

VIVIPAROUS SNAIL
The viviparous
banded snail,
which has one of
the largest shells of
European freshwater
snails, gives birth to
live young.

Ram's-horn
shell

Giant African
river snail

Land snails

In order to survive, land snails need to remain moist, so they are usually most active at night or when it is cloudy or rainy. In dry conditions many types of snail can remain totally inactive for long periods, thereby retaining both energy and moisture. One museum specimen—thought to be long dead—was removed from a display case for cleaning, and began to move out of its shell after several years of "hibernation".

PICKY EATER
Snails are pests in gardens and feed on most types of vegetation, including many of the same plants humans do, such as lettuce.

COLORFUL CUBAN COLLECTIBLES
The brightly colored Cuban land snail is now protected by law because over-collecting has threatened the species' future.

Cuban land snails

REGIONAL RARITY
This extremely rare tropidophora snail is only found on the island of Madagascar in the Indian Ocean.

Operculum (p. 32)

Teeth

UPSIDE-DOWN SNAIL
This unusual snail from the South American rain forest grows with its spiral facing earthward.

SNAILS IN TREES
These bright-green snails are only found on Manus Island in the Pacific and are on the official list of endangered species.

Manus land snails

Growth scar

Left-handed São Tomé snail

LEFT-HANDED SNAIL
Shells that coil in a counter-clockwise direction are known as sinistral, or left-handed, shells—a feature that is relatively common among land snails.

Achatina snail

MASSIVE PEST
The large achatina snails occur naturally in Africa, where they are eaten, but are viewed as pests in other parts of the tropics, where they have been introduced by people.

European striped snails

Common garden snails

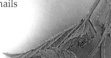

COMMONER IN THE GARDEN
Although abundant in gardens, snails do less harm than their cousins, the slugs.

BANDING TOGETHER
The common European striped snail has a very variable pattern. The color and number of bands differ according to the kind of environment occupied by the snails (p. 41).

Homes with hinges

BIVALVES ARE AMONG THE BEST KNOWN of all marine creatures. Like the gastropods, bivalves are mollusks, but their shells are divided into two parts, or valves, that completely enclose and protect the soft body of the mollusk inside. The valves are connected by a shelly ridge or teeth that form a hinge and can be opened and closed by strong muscles and ligaments. Compared to the gastropods, bivalves do not lead very active lives—unable to extend far out of their shells to crawl, many live embedded in sand and mud (p. 42) or remain hidden in rock crevices, while others attach themselves to a hard surface. Bivalves feed by opening their valves and filtering water through their gills to catch tiny creatures in the water around them. Bivalves can occur in vast numbers: some areas of the seafloor contain as many as 8,000 living shells of one type in an area of 10 square feet (1 sq meter).

THE BIRTH OF VENUS
This detail from the famous painting by Botticelli shows Venus being born from a scallop shell.

Royal cloak scallop

SCURRYING SCALLOPS
Scallops are among the best-known bivalve mollusks. Some scallops have the ability to open and close their valves to swim away rapidly when disturbed.

Pacific thorny oyster

SPINY OYSTER SHELL
Spiny, or thorny, oysters are also known as chrysanthemum shells because of their likeness to the spiky-petaled flowers. Although not related to the true oyster, they are similar in that they remain attached to a solid base throughout their lives.

Ligament

BUTTERFLY WINGS
Shiny, colorful tellin shells are frequently washed ashore still in pairs, often resembling butterfly wings.

Flat tellin

Thin tellin

Toothed donax, also called a bean clam

BEAN CLAMS
Generally tiny and wedge-shaped, these creatures live in large numbers on warm-water beaches. Being so abundant, they are often used as food, especially in soups.

Noble
pen shell

SHELLY BATHTUB
The huge tridacna shell houses an animal that can feed up to 20 people! Common in the Molucca Islands, here it is being used as a child's bathtub.

THE GIANT PEN SHELL
The pinna, or pen shell, spends its life in an upright position with its tapered end semiembedded in soft bases, usually among weeds. The giant pen shell, which lives in the Mediterranean, is one of the largest bivalve mollusks, occasionally reaching a length of 2 ft (60 cm).

OPEN AND SHUT CASE
Bivalves spend much of their lives with their valves slightly apart, and they must be able to close the gap quickly and securely to protect themselves from predators. For this purpose, the two halves of a bivalve shell match perfectly and, when shut, the opening can be just as hard to penetrate as the rest of the shell.

Cockscomb oyster

Spiny
sand cockle

Fluted
giant clam

Baby noble
pen shell

MINIATURE MAN-EATER
There are many different types and sizes of clam, but the biggest of all shelled mollusks is the giant clam, whose valves can measure 4 ft (1.2 m) and weigh more than 500 lb (225 kg). These huge shells have been put to many uses, including bathtubs and feeding troughs, and the shell is so strong that it can be made into ax heads with which to fell trees. It is believed that the giant clam can trap and kill pearl divers but, in reality, its valves close too slowly to be dangerous to humans.

Byssal threads are secreted by some bivalves to anchor themselves to a hard base

Strange seashells

Most seashells are either gastropods (p. 10) or bivalves (p. 16), but there are a few other types of shelled creature that show little resemblance to either group. The smallest and least-known mollusk group is the gastroverms—rare creatures with small, limpet-shaped shells that can live 3 miles (5 km) below the surface of the sea. Better known are the chitons, sometimes referred to as coat-of-mail shells because the shells are made up of eight separate plates. Scaphopods, or tusk shells as they are commonly called, have shells that look like elephants' tusks. Like the chitons, these mollusks are primitive creatures that can be found in most of the world's oceans, even in shallow water. The most advanced of all the mollusks are the cephalopods (from the Greek words for "head" and "foot")—so called because of their distinctive tentacled heads. This class includes the octopus, squid, cuttlefish, and nautilus—mostly free-swimming creatures that have evolved without true shells.

Olive chitons

Shelly plates

Individual valves of a chiton

Girdle

PARTS OF A CHITON
The shell of a chiton consists of eight plates, or valves, which are attached to the back of the soft-bodied animal. These valves are joined and surrounded by a stretchy muscular band known as a girdle, allowing the animal to move over irregular surfaces. When a chiton is detached from its ground, it curls up to protect its soft body.

HOLDING ON TIGHT
Chitons are found living on solid objects such as rocks and other shells. Like limpets, they hold on tight to the surface when disturbed.

SIZEABLE VARIETY
There are more than 950 species of chiton known and, although they are all roughly the same shape, they can vary greatly in size, from a fraction of an inch (0.25 cm) to more than 12 in (30 cm) long.

Underside of a chiton shell

TUSK SHELLS
Tusk shells live with their heads buried in sand or mud. They feed on microscopic organisms that they catch and pass to their mouth with club-shaped tentacles.

Shell

Feeding tentacles

Foot

Mantle

Common tusk shells

Eight sensory and feeding arms

VALUABLE ASSETS
The ivory tusks of elephants have always been highly prized, but tusk shells, too, were once valuable. Like the famed money cowries (p. 13) once used as currency in Africa and the South Pacific, strings of tusk shells were used as money and jewelry by some Native American peoples.

Elephant's tusk shell

Two tentacles are longer

Green tusk shells

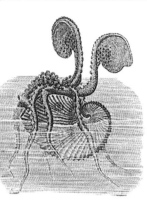

MYTHICAL SAILOR
It was once believed that the argonaut, or paper nautilus, "sailed" along using its shell as a boat and two of its arms as sails. However, this is not true; indeed, the wafer-thin "shell" is actually an egg case used by the female argonaut and discarded after her eggs hatch.

Paper nautilus

Chambered nautilus shell

CHAMBERED NAUTILUS
The nautilus is the only cephalopod with a true external shell, but the animal lives only in the outer compartment. The inside of the shell is divided into many pearly chambers that are filled with gas and help the nautilus to float. Buoyancy is controlled by taking in or letting out water.

INTERNAL SHELL
Over millions of years the external shell of the colorful cuttlefishes evolved into internal "cuttlebones".

Living common cuttlefish

SQUID
The squid's internal shell is a thin, transparent tube that supports the animal's streamlined body. The squid propels itself backward by jet propulsion, taking in and squirting out water, and can escape from danger by letting out a cloud of ink to hide its movements.

Long-finned squid

Common spirula

Spirula shells

SPIRAL SHELL
The coiled shell of the spirula has a chambered interior like that seen in the nautilus (above), but this creature is more closely related to the cuttlefish, its shell being inside the animal's body.

GIANTS OF THE DEEP
Sailors' tales of enormous sea monsters were probably based on sightings of huge cephalopods. The giant squid is the largest of all invertebrate animals, and the biggest one ever found was 59 ft (18 m) long.

Urchins of the sea

THE SEA URCHINS belong to a large group of creatures called echinoderms, a word derived from the Greek words for "spiny" and "skin." Various types of odd-looking creatures with strange-sounding names belong to this group, which includes the starfishes and the sea cucumbers, although the sea urchins, sea potatoes, sea biscuits, and sand dollars are the only ones with shells. There are some 800 types of sea urchin living on the bottom of the world's oceans today. Ancient in origin, they have adapted to most kinds of marine environment, from the polar regions to the tropics. They can be found in shallow or very deep water and are omnivores that feed on algae, small animals, and decaying matter. Echinoderm bodies often show a five-rayed symmetry (evenness), a feature that is particularly clear in starfish-type animals.

Tropical sea urchin tests

SEA URCHIN TESTS
The shell of a sea urchin is known as a test and is made up of a series of plates that join each other or sometimes overlap. The test encloses and protects the soft parts of the animal. It is often shaped like a slightly flattened ball and usually divided into five main areas. Sea urchin tests are often very colorful and range in size from less than ½ in (1 cm) to more than 6 in (15 cm) in diameter.

The smallest urchins of Europe's seas, these pea urchins are commonly found in beach debris

SPIKY OR SPINELESS?
When alive, sea urchins are covered with numerous spines and tube feet that help them to move around. The spines are secured to the test by muscles around raised areas on the shell, which form a "ball-and-socket" joint that allows the spines to move in all directions. The spines on a sea urchin are used for locomotion, protection, and sometimes even as digging tools to burrow into rocks.

Sea urchin with all its spines

The edible sea urchin, the largest of Europe's urchins

Sea urchin test exposed when spines removed

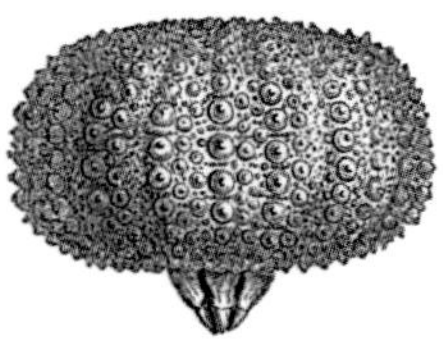

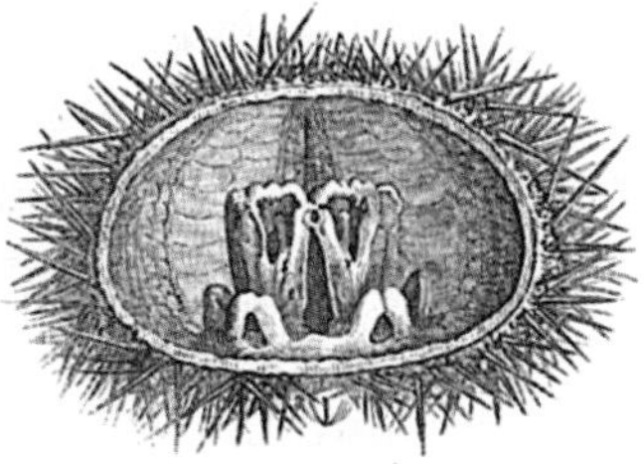

EATING URCHIN

Urchins feed with the aid of a complex, five-toothed jaw that resembles the part of an electric drill that grips the drill bit. The jaw is made up of bony plates operated by muscles and is often referred to as "Aristotle's lantern" because of its similarity to certain types of old oil lamp. The mouth of a sea urchin is on the underside of the test and always faces toward the seabed.

"Aristotle's lantern," or jaw parts of sea urchin

Atlantic cidaris urchin

THE LONG AND THE SHORT OF IT

Cidaris sea urchins often have a lot of very tiny spines, together with a few longer, thicker ones. This type lives in fairly deep water and can be found in the Atlantic Ocean and the Mediterranean Sea.

SLATE PENCIL SEA URCHIN

This type of sea urchin is commonly found on tropical coral reefs, where it tends to hide in crevices during the day, coming out to feed at night. The extremely long and heavy spines are sometimes used as wind chimes or as jewelry.

BURIED TREASURE?

Sand dollars form a distinctive group of sea urchins that have adapted to life on sandy shores. Unlike other sea urchins, they have tiny spines and a flattened shape that improves their stability on the seabed and makes it easy for them to make shallow burrows in the sand. Sand dollars live in warm waters and are especially common in the Caribbean and Australian seas.

Indo-Pacific slate pencil sea urchin

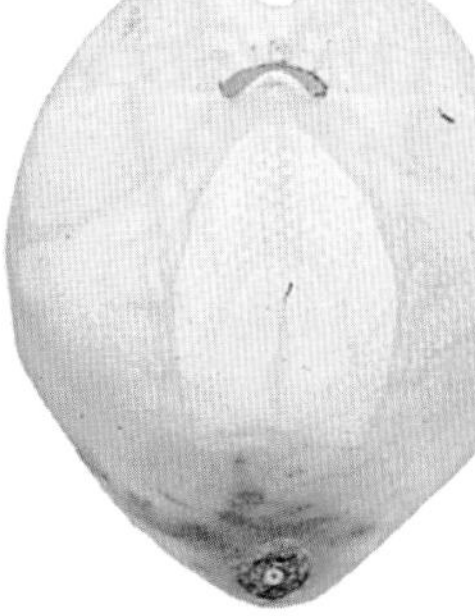

Sea potato with spines removed

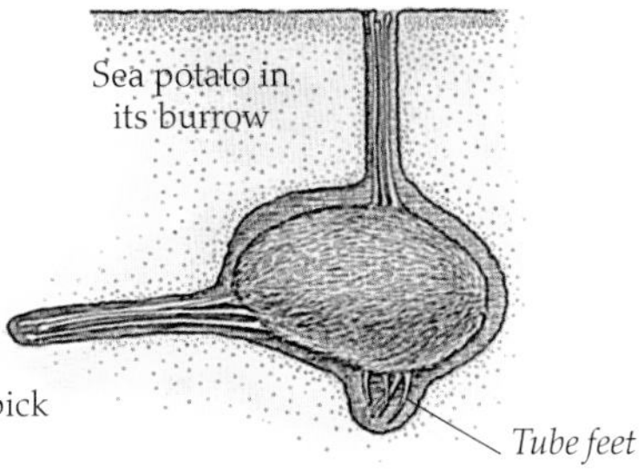

Sea potato with spines

THE SEA POTATO

Like the sand dollar, the sea potato, or heart urchin, is adapted to live in sandy environments but often burrows down to 8 in (20 cm) deep. The sea potato has modified, extra-long tube feet that it can extend to pick up food from the surface of the sand.

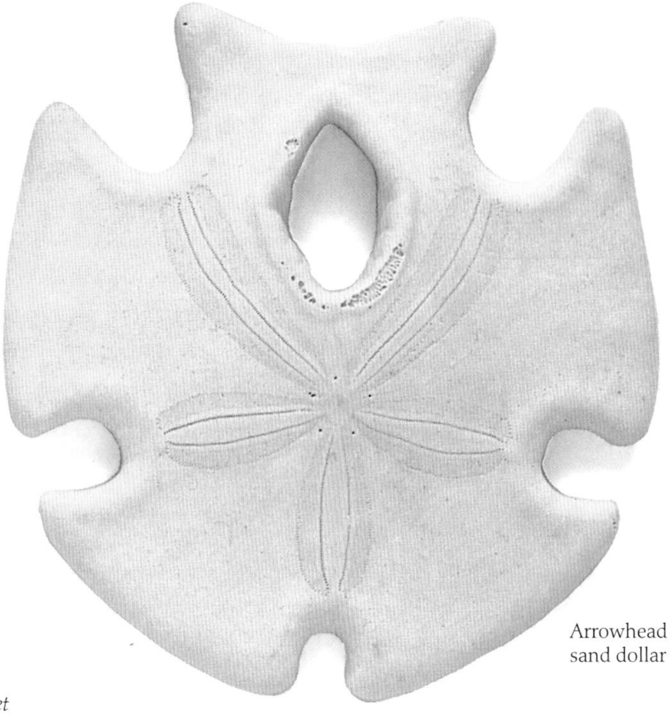

Sea potato in its burrow

Tube feet

Arrowhead sand dollar

Armor-plated animals

WHILE MANY CREATURES HAVE DEVELOPED strong outer casings that we call shells, one group has evolved what is more like a very hard and thick layer of skin. This large group is called the crustaceans, of which there are more than 70,000 different types—including lobsters, crabs, and crayfish—mostly living in the sea. Most crustaceans possess shells that are jointed—like the suits of armor worn by medieval knights. Crustaceans belong to the group known as the arthropods—the largest group of living creatures—which includes all insects. Arthropods share many similarities, including segmented bodies, jointed limbs, and the hardened outer skeleton, or shell, that is shed from time to time to allow the animal to grow.

THE LOBSTER IN ART
Lobsters have pleased food lovers and inspired artists as well. This detail is from a 17th-century painting, *Still Life with Lobster*, by Joris Van Son.

Tailpiece, or telson

Abdomen divided into six segments, or somites

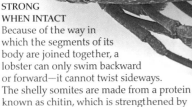

STRONG WHEN INTACT
Because of the way in which the segments of its body are joined together, a lobster can only swim backward or forward—it cannot twist sideways. The shelly somites are made from a protein known as chitin, which is strengthened by deposits of calcium salts. The somites are much softer at the joints, to allow the animal to move. In order to grow, the lobster must occasionally shed its shell and grow a new one. This makes it extremely vulnerable to enemies, and the lobster wisely hides away until its new shell has had time to harden.

COPYCAT CASING
Like the lobster, the knights of old sacrificed flexibility in return for a protective suit of armor.

First leg, or cheliped

Carapace

THE ARMOR EXPLORED
Most crustaceans have a segmented,
or jointed, body at some time or other
in their lives. Lobsters and shrimp
show this segmentation clearly as
adults. The bodies of these animals
are made up of a series of shelly,
overlapping rings with attached
appendages (limbs). In lobsters there
are 19 such rings, or somites. The tip
of the head and the tailpiece are not
regarded as somites, since they do
not have any true appendages.

Antennule

Eye

Antenna

Maxilliped

Moveable
finger, or claw

Ambulatory, or walking, legs

Fixed finger

23

Shells with 10 legs

PERHAPS THE MOST familiar crustaceans are crabs, lobsters, shrimp, and crayfish. They all have the characteristic hardened, jointed shells, and 10 legs, giving them the collective name of "decapods." But within the group crustacea, there is so much variety that it is impossible to find one feature common to every creature in the group that separates it from all other animals. The members of the group range from tiny water fleas that live mainly in freshwater, to ostracods with their glow-in-the-dark bodies (p. 54); parasitic and limpetlike copepods, sometimes known as fish lice, that attach themselves firmly to their hosts; and even the heavily armored barnacles. Many of these creatures are microscopic and form a large part of plankton—the drifting life of the oceans. Plankton occurs in huge numbers in the world's oceans and is an important part of the marine food chain, eaten by creatures that range in size from tiny mollusks to huge whales.

ALIVE AND SWIMMING
Crab larvae, like the common crab larva above, are free-swimming. A new hatchling is not much bigger than the tip of a pencil and looks more like a mosquito than a crab.

MEAN FIDDLER
Called the fiddler crab because the enlarged claw of the male is held in a position similar to that in which a musician holds a fiddle, this creature lives in sandy burrows and sandy mud.

Large claw is used to frighten enemies

Pincer claws used for catching and holding prey as well as for defense

NO WAY OUT
Fishing for crabs and lobsters simply involves setting traps and waiting. The crab or lobster pots usually have two holes that get smaller toward the center of the basket. Crabs and lobsters, attracted by the bait within, crawl in and then are unable to get out and have no choice but to await their fate.

19th-century engraving showing a crab and lobster fishing scene on a beach

A NEW SUIT
Crabs, like all crustaceans, must shed their skins, or molt, in order to grow. At the time of molting, cracks appear in a crab's shell, and the creature's soft parts begin to come through, gradually pushing aside the old shell. Crabs in the process of molting are called peelers by fishermen. When caught, peelers are kept in tanks until they have molted, so that they can be sold as "soft-shells"—a delicacy for the gourmet. Soft-shells usually eat their old shells, as the land crab on the right is demonstrating.

Pointed feet help crab to dig under sand

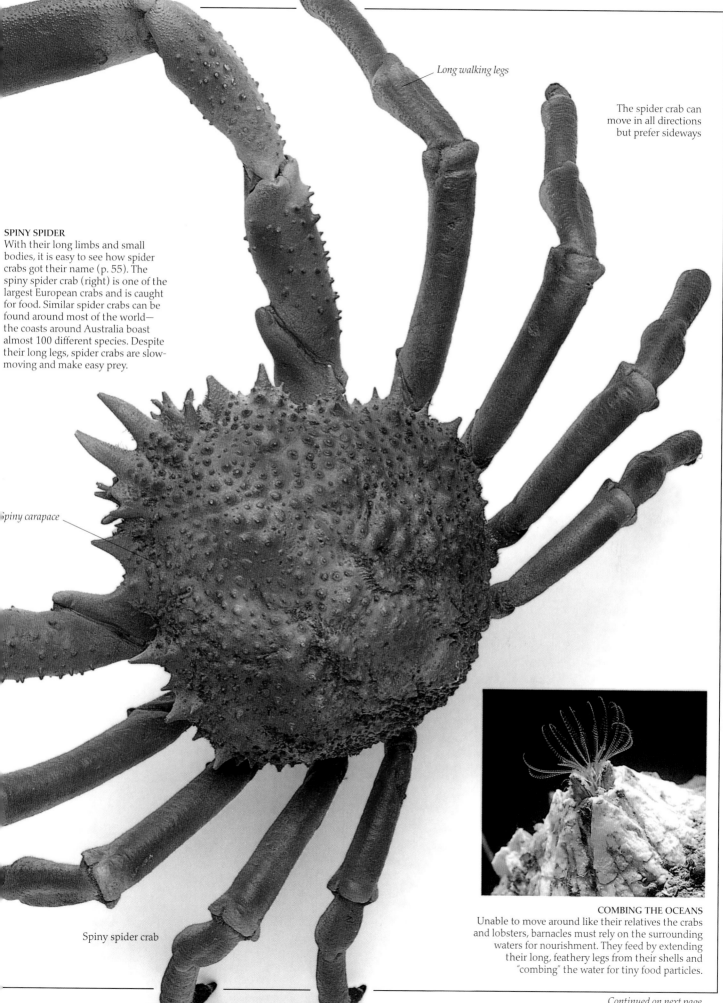

Long walking legs

The spider crab can
move in all directions
but prefer sideways

SPINY SPIDER
With their long limbs and small
bodies, it is easy to see how spider
crabs got their name (p. 55). The
spiny spider crab (right) is one of the
largest European crabs and is caught
for food. Similar spider crabs can be
found around most of the world—
the coasts around Australia boast
almost 100 different species. Despite
their long legs, spider crabs are slow-
moving and make easy prey.

Spiny carapace

Spiny spider crab

COMBING THE OCEANS
Unable to move around like their relatives the crabs
and lobsters, barnacles must rely on the surrounding
waters for nourishment. They feed by extending
their long, feathery legs from their shells and
"combing" the water for tiny food particles.

Continued on next page

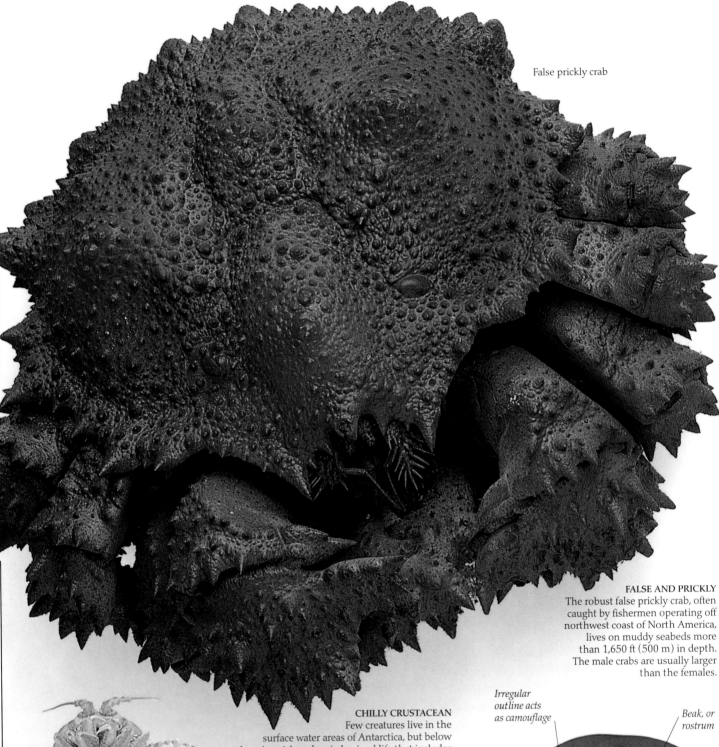

False prickly crab

FALSE AND PRICKLY
The robust false prickly crab, often caught by fishermen operating off northwest coast of North America, lives on muddy seabeds more than 1,650 ft (500 m) in depth. The male crabs are usually larger than the females.

CHILLY CRUSTACEAN
Few creatures live in the surface water areas of Antarctica, but below there is a rich and varied animal life that includes many crustaceans. The Antarctic isopod is a primitive crustacean that lives in shallow waters beneath the ice. Most isopods are small, but some grow to over 14 in (35 cm) in length.

Irregular outline acts as camouflage

Beak, or rostrum

Antarctic isopod

Live Antarctic isopod

UMBRELLA CRAB
Like the false prickly crab, the turtle or umbrella crab (above) lives off the northwest coast of the US and Canada and is especially common off the cold-water coasts of British Columbia in Canada. Its shape and color help it to blend in with the seaweed on which it lives and feeds. It can remain completely motionless when enemies are near.

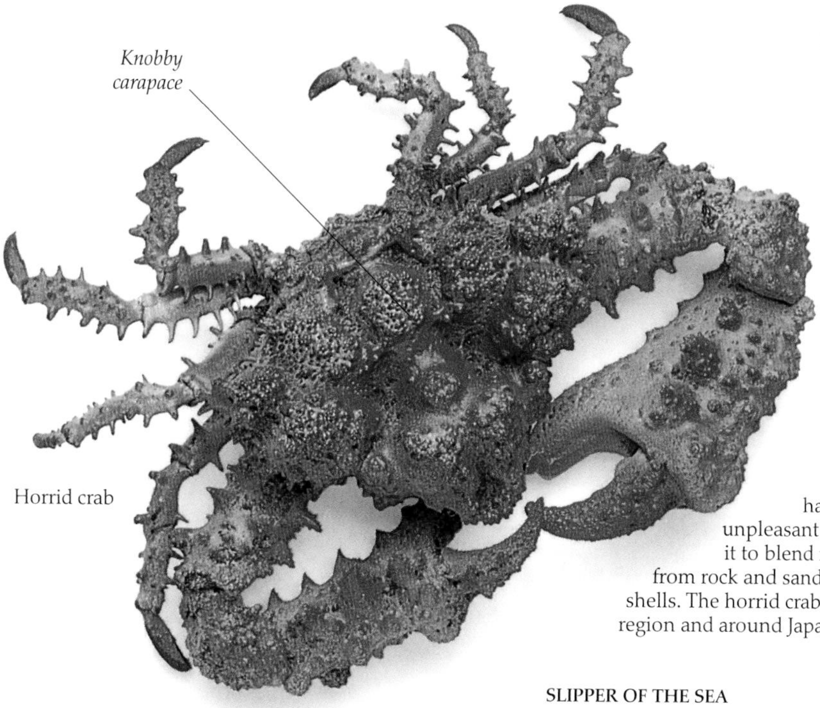

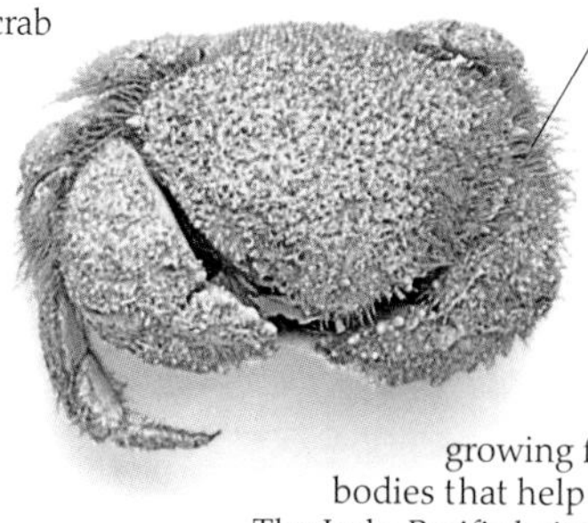

Knobby carapace

Indo-Pacific hairy crab

Legs fold under body for protection

HAIRY SHELL
Many types of crab have hairs growing from their shelled bodies that help with camouflage. The Indo-Pacific hairy crab is a resident of rocky shores. When curled up, it looks more like an algae-covered stone than a crab.

Horrid crab

A HORRID SIGHT
The lumpy, uneven shell of this crab has earned it the name "horrid crab." Its unpleasant appearance, however, probably helps it to blend in with its surroundings, which range from rock and sandy mud to seabeds made up of broken shells. The horrid crab is well distributed in the Indo-Pacific region and around Japan, where it is known as *karmishigami*.

SLIPPER OF THE SEA
So called because of their flattened appearance, slipper lobsters live in most seas, including the icy waters of the Arctic. The species shown here is a common inhabitant of muddy seabeds throughout much of the Indo-Pacific. It is fished and eaten in many parts of the world, and is very popular in Australia.

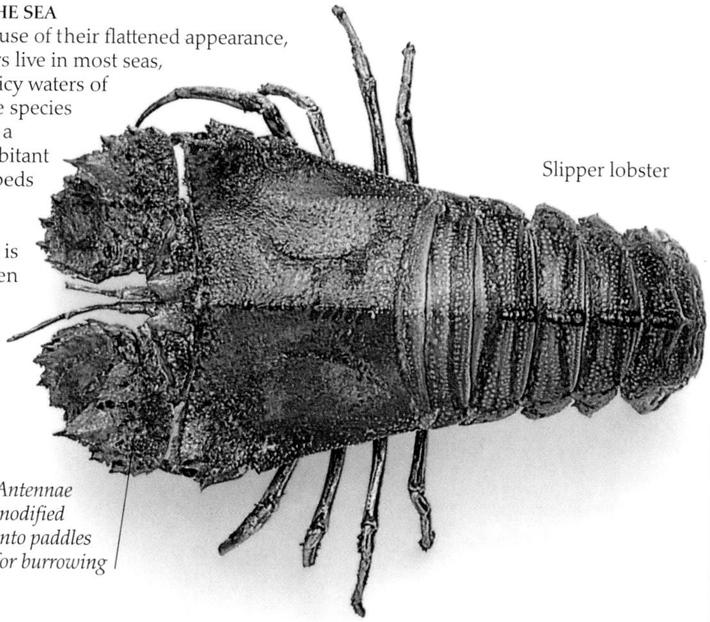

Slipper lobster

A GOOD COVER-UP
Many crustaceans are able to cover themselves with material such as seaweed in order to remain hidden in their habitat. The crab above, standing on deadmen's fingers (a type of soft coral), is adorned with a starfish. In this case, however, the camouflage is unintended—the starfish probably crawled up on the crab's head by itself.

Antennae modified into paddles for burrowing

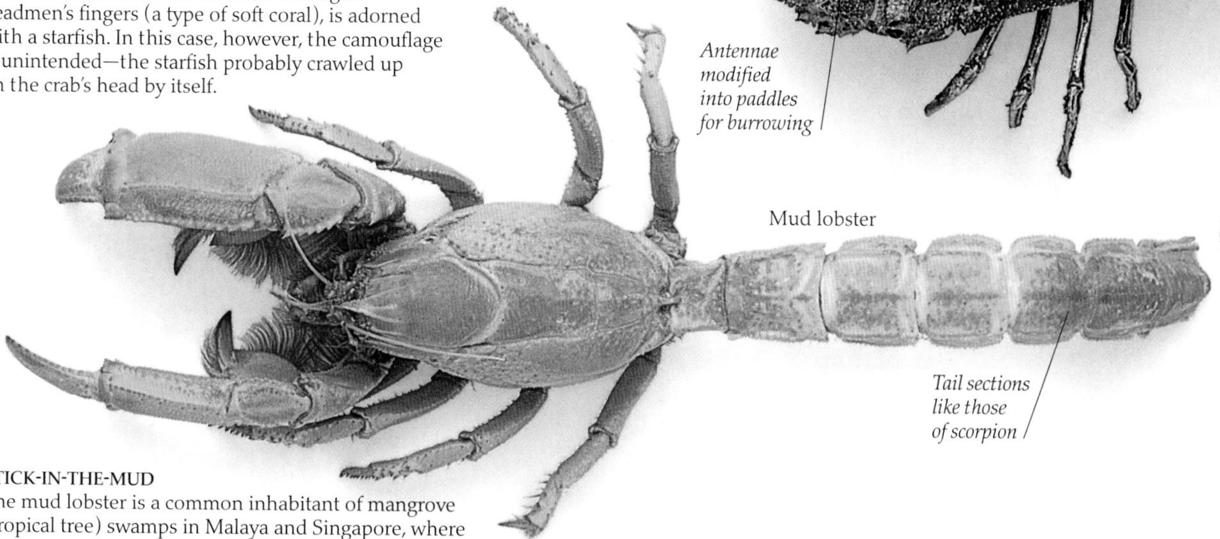

Mud lobster

Tail sections like those of scorpion

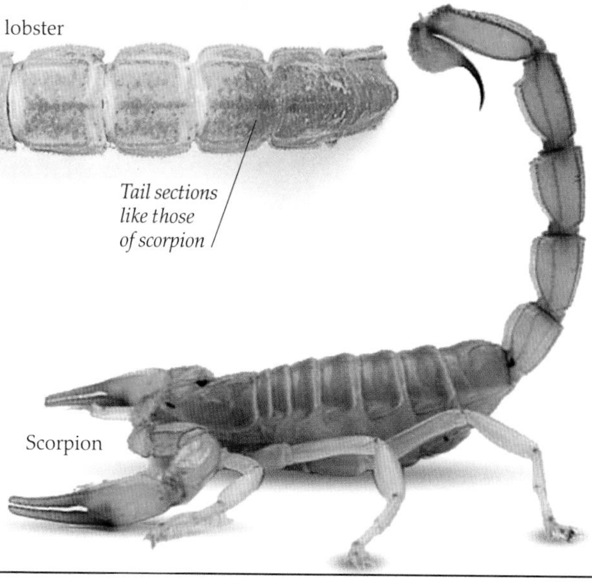

STICK-IN-THE-MUD
The mud lobster is a common inhabitant of mangrove (tropical tree) swamps in Malaya and Singapore, where it lives buried under the mud. Although seldom seen, even at night, the mud lobster gives its presence away by the distinctive mounds it makes in the mud. Comparing this lobster with the scorpion (right), it is easy to see why scorpions have long been thought to be related to the crustaceans.

Scorpion

Turtles, tortoises, and terrapins

TURTLES, TORTOISES, AND TERRAPINS form an ancient and closely related family, having lived on this planet since the age of the dinosaurs. Being reptiles, they are vertebrates like us, but are unique in the animal kingdom in that they have a solid outer shell as well as an internal skeleton. They are also cold-blooded creatures, unable to regulate their body temperature internally. They can, however, raise their body temperature by basking in the sun. Most tortoises in the wild tend to live in the warmer parts of the world. Tortoises can be found in colder areas, too, but they then need to hibernate during the winter months. Although they seem very similar, tortoises, turtles, and terrapins have evolved in different environments: tortoises usually live on land, terrapins in freshwater, and all turtles but one live in the sea.

THE HARE AND THE TORTOISE
Tortoises are famous for their slow movements, but as the well-known fable "The Hare and the Tortoise" tells us, determination is more important than speed. Despite its slowness, the tortoise has managed to survive on Earth with very little change for over 250 million years, relying mainly on its hard shell for protection.

Stinkpot turtle

Red-eared slider

Painted turtle

BASKING TERRAPINS
Terrapins live in freshwater habitats and can often be seen basking in the sunshine on rocks or riverbanks. Usually smaller than either tortoises or turtles, these little creatures are often kept as pets in freshwater tanks.

Clawed foot

Scutes, or scales, cover bony carapace

On the Galápagos Islands in the Pacific live "giant" tortoises that can reach about 5 ft (1.5 m) in length.

Plastron

TORTOISE TALE
The armor-plated tortoise has a distinctive domed shell, or carapace, on top and a flat, bony plate, called a plastron, below. This plate protects most of the animal's soft tissues and its exposed legs and head can be drawn quickly inside the shell when danger threatens. The tortoise does not have teeth but can still inflict a painful bite with the aid of its strong jaws and the sharp, horny tissue that surrounds them, like the beak of a bird.

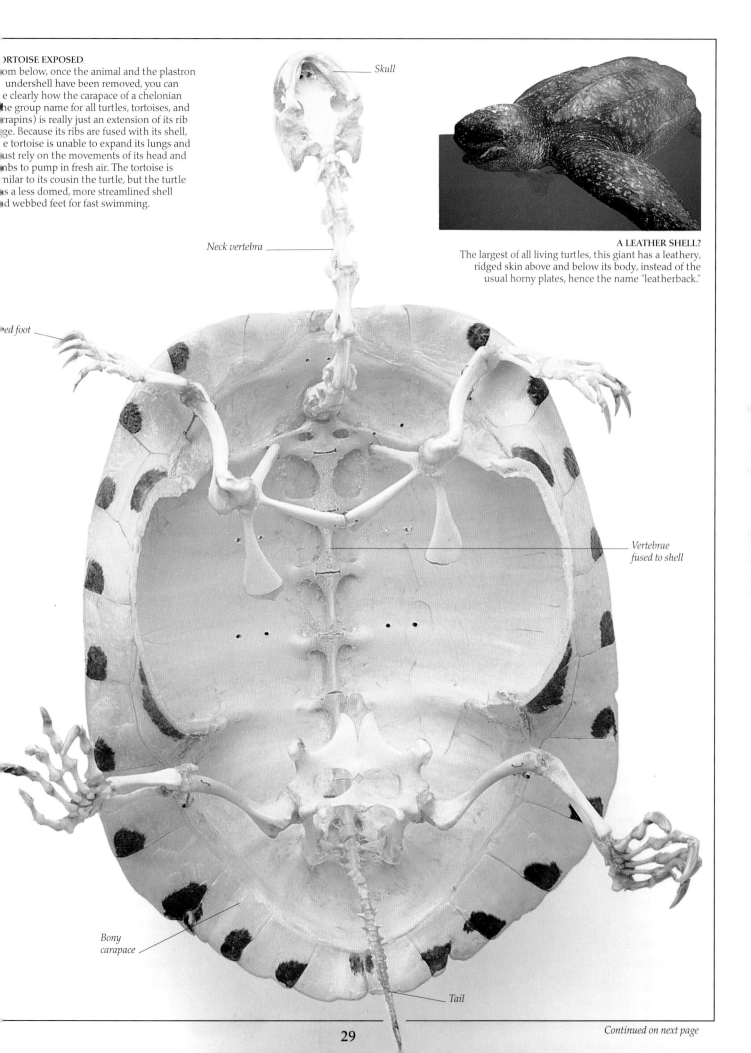

TORTOISE EXPOSED
From below, once the animal and the plastron or undershell have been removed, you can see clearly how the carapace of a chelonian (the group name for all turtles, tortoises, and terrapins) is really just an extension of its rib cage. Because its ribs are fused with its shell, the tortoise is unable to expand its lungs and must rely on the movements of its head and limbs to pump in fresh air. The tortoise is similar to its cousin the turtle, but the turtle has a less domed, more streamlined shell and webbed feet for fast swimming.

Skull

Neck vertebra

A LEATHER SHELL?
The largest of all living turtles, this giant has a leathery, ridged skin above and below its body, instead of the usual horny plates, hence the name "leatherback."

Webbed foot

Vertebrae fused to shell

Bony carapace

Tail

Continued on next page

Tortoiseshell patterns

There are more than 300 different types of tortoise, turtle, and terrapin, all belonging to a reptilian group called the chelonians. Although the structure of the shell is essentially the same in most of the creatures in this group, the markings on the bony scales that make up the carapace are often very distinctive and provide a useful means of identification. As with many living creatures, the coloration of young specimens is different to that of adults.

MOCK TURTLE
In Lewis Carroll's story *Alice's Adventures in Wonderland*, Alice encounters many strange creatures on her travels, one of which is the melancholy Mock Turtle. Encouraged by the Gryphon, the Mock Turtle teaches Alice how to dance the famous Lobster Quadrille, and tearfully laments the fact that he is not a true turtle. This leads him to sing "Turtle Soup," a sad reminder that his days are numbered.

Young leopard tortoise carapace

Juvenile leopard tortoise carapace

LEOPARD BY NAME, TORTOISE BY NATURE
The leopard tortoise gets its name from the speckled markings on its domed shell. The young shells (above and left) have not yet developed the distinctive pattern visible on the adult (far left). Although widely distributed on the African continent, the leopard tortoise prefers savanna and woodland areas, where it feeds on a variety of plants.

AN EXTRA WEIGHT
As if the weight of its own enormous shell was not enough to carry, this giant tortoise is also bearing the load of Lord Walter Rothschild, the world-famous 19th-century naturalist. Giant tortoises were first discovered by Charles Darwin on his voyage to the Galápagos Islands, and they have fascinated naturalists ever since. Lord Rothschild was especially fond of these slow-moving creatures and kept many at his museum in Tring, England.

Main carapace color is brown

Mature leopard tortoise carapace

Hawksbill turtles

One of the best known of all marine turtles is the hawksbill. Once hunted for its beautiful shell (right), this turtle is now on the official list of critically endangered species and imports are banned in many countries. It can be found in most warm seas around the world, where it feeds on mollusks and crustaceans.

Natural hawksbill tortoiseshell

Thick overlapping plates

Flipperlike limb

19th-century "lorgnette" glasses made from tortoiseshell

1920s tortoiseshell box

19th-century tortoiseshell hair comb

GLIDING WITH EASE
Hawksbill turtles are extremely fast swimmers, their long, paddlelike flippers and low shells helping them to glide smoothly through the water. Marine turtles come ashore to lay their eggs, and on land they are even slower than tortoises.

TORTOISESHELL TREASURES
During the late 19th and early 20th centuries, it was fashionable to own objects sculpted from tortoiseshell. The most beautiful tortoiseshell comes from the hawksbill turtle.

A growing shell

Common European oyster

Growth rings

As a mollusk grows, the shell in which it lives grows too. By steadily depositing crystals of calcium carbonate onto a framework of protein, called conchiolin, a hard shell is created so that the soft creature is always protected. The part of the mollusk that makes these secretions is a sheet of soft tissue called the mantle, which is located between the shell itself and the inner organs that it encloses. If you examine the lip of a live shell, you can often detect a thin, flexible layer of developing shelly matter—it is at this point that a shell is most vulnerable, and many mollusks have therefore developed a trap door, called an operculum, to protect the exposed part of the body. Many mollusks pause between periods of growth, creating a shell of varying thicknesses. These growth marks, or rings, are very evident in some shells, such as oysters, and are often so regular that they become a reliable means of identifying the species.

np
lm
p
r
ts
mp
lm

OYSTER GROWTH RINGS
An oyster shell develops from a minute spawn—only ½ in (2 mm) long—that settles on a hard surface after about two weeks of drifting and begins to develop a shell. Adult oysters can grow to more than 6 in (15 cm) in diameter, but many are fished for food long before they reach old age. Many oysters have characteristic growth rings on their top valves, like those seen in a sliced tree trunk.

STEADY GROWTH
As a tortoise grows, so does its shell. The bony plates that make up the shell are just an extension of the tortoise's skeleton.

THE DEVELOPING SHELL
As with many mollusks, the triton develops from a microscopic larva, known as a veliger. After varying degrees of time, the larva will settle to develop a shell—in some tritons, this can take a year and means that larvae from the same mother may end up separated by hundreds of miles. The young shell of a triton bears little resemblance to the adult form, each whorl bringing with it some new color or variation in shape. As with the oyster, there are distinct growth marks, although here the growth stages are marked by a thickening of the lip at each stage, and in the adult shell, these can be seen as pronounced ridges known as varices. When a mollusk reaches old age, it does not add new whorls but continues to lay down calcium salts, which thicken its existing shell.

The early, more fragile whorls do not contain mollusk tissues and are often broken off or eroded over the years

As the shell ages, the brightly colored juvenile whorls start to fade

Juvenile shell

Adult coloration and ridging begin to appear

Lip is always fine in young shells

At each new whorl of the spiral, the mollusk pauses to thicken its aperture (opening)

A HERMIT AND ITS HOME
Unlike most mollusks, crustaceans outgrow their shells and so shed them. Their outer layer hardens to form the new shell. They need to build several completely new casings throughout their lives (p. 22). Most crabs are totally protected by a hard outer shell, but the hermit crab has a relatively soft body and adopts an old mollusk shell as a portable protective shelter. As it grows, the crab discards its shell and goes in search of a bigger home.

Hook by which crab secures itself inside other shells

Great hermit crab inside an old Neapolitan triton shell

The characteristic lip thickenings of earlier growth stages are known as varices

As the whorls get larger, the spiral ridges become more pronounced

The fully developed shell is very heavy and its coloration is much stronger

An almost adult shell that is ready to develop its characteristic teeth and coloring within the aperture

Shells for food lovers

As a food resource, the sea offers an incredibly varied menu. In addition to fish, lobsters, and crabs, sea urchins and most mollusks are eaten all around the world. Many people who live near the sea survive almost entirely on seafood, and it is true that these are often the healthiest people—most seafood being rich in protein but low in calories. It is rather strange that many people shy away from the French delicacy of snails, but are quite happy to eat squid or a plate of spaghetti marinara, filled with small clams. Bivalve shells are the most popular form of shellfish; varieties of oyster, clam, scallop, cockle, and mussel are found in many parts of the world, and several types are farmed solely for human consumption. Some gastropods are also very popular; abalones are sometimes eaten as steak in parts of North America, Japan, and Australia, as are queen conches throughout the Caribbean. In Europe, the whelk, a marine snail, is often fished commercially. For the shell collector, the fish market is often the best place to find local shells, especially in tropical areas.

THE WALRUS AND THE CARPENTER
In the Lewis Carroll story *Through the Looking-Glass*, the Walrus and the Carpenter ask some young oysters to take a stroll along the beach, and then proceed to eat the oysters with bread and butter!

Hinge
ligament

THE POPULAR CLAM
Often used in soups and sauces, this small but abundant clam is found in great quantities in the seas of northern Europe. Its American cousin, a much larger but otherwise very similar bivalve called the Atlantic surf clam, is a major food source; some 45 million lb (20 million kg) of its meat are fished each year between Nova Scotia and North Carolina.

OYSTER CATCHER
With its long, sharp beak, the oyster catcher is well equipped for digging bivalves from the sand.

"ALIVE, ALIVE-O"
Among the most popular of all edible mollusks is the oyster—each ocean has its own varieties, some more than double the size of these live Portuguese oysters. The traditional method of eating oysters is to swallow them whole, straight from the shell, uncooked, and complete with all the natural juices. In the past, it was not uncommon to see street vendors serving live oysters to be eaten on the spot.

Oysters being sold in a street market

Mantle tissue

Adductor muscle tissue

Portuguese oysters

Common
cockle

Hinge

*Exhalant
siphon*

Foot

MOUTH-WATERING MUSSELS
Easily found in fish markets and very tasty, mussels can
be cooked and served with the open shell in
a variety of sauces or used in soups—the most
popular dish is probably the French *moules
marinières*. In Europe and North
America, most mussels are
usually blue; the green
New Zealand
variety shown
here is exported
throughout
the world.

HEART
OF A COCKLE
The small body of the common cockle
is made up of all the same parts as the
larger shellfish. Like most other seafood, cockles
are best eaten fresh, but can also be found
pickled in jars. The pickling process
preserves the meat and
keeps it from spoiling.

*Inhalant
siphon*

Gills

New Zealand
mussel

*Adductor
muscle*

*Byssus, or
byssal threads,
anchor shell to
solid ground*

Hinge ligament

BREAKING AND ENTERING
Mollusks are an important
source of food for many creatures
other than humans. The California
sea otter tugs abalones and
other mollusks from their underwater
homes and uses a rock to smash open
the shells as it lies on its back in the water.

A NATURAL DISH
The distinctively shaped shell of a
scallop makes a natural dish on which
to serve scallop meat. One of the most
common varieties has one flat valve and
one concave, or dish-shaped, valve. In
Europe, the entire mollusk is
usually eaten; in North
America only the
white muscle
is used.

*White
muscle tissue*

Flatter
upper valve

Concave lower valve
containing mollusk

A pearl is born

ALTHOUGH THEY ARE HIGHLY PRIZED by humans, pearls begin their lives as a nuisance to the creatures that make them. If a foreign body—such as a tiny piece of rock or the egg of a parasite—becomes lodged between the mantle of a mollusk and its shell, the animal will cover the object with layers of shelly material, or nacre, and create a pearl. In the case of pearl oyster shells, which have a rainbowlike interior, the pearls that are formed are as beautiful and lustrous as the inside of the shell. All types of mollusk are capable of producing pearls; bivalves are more likely to do so because they tend to live in a fixed position and are unable to extend out of their shells to dislodge a foreign body. Naturally formed pearls are extremely rare, but a way of cultivating pearls artificially was perfected by the Japanese at the start of the 20th century, making cheaper pearls more accessible. By inserting an artificial nucleus into a living oyster, a good-size "cultured" pearl is virtually guaranteed after three to five years. The pearl industry is now so large that around 500 million pearls are produced each year.

PEARLY BUDDHAS

Although the Japanese are credited with perfecting the process of pearl cultivation, the Chinese had discovered pearlification and put it to use more than 700 years before. Little clay figures of the Buddha were inserted inside freshwater mussels and left for about a year, after which the shells would be opened to reveal perfectly coated mother-of-pearl figurines. Some mussels have been preserved with the tiny Buddhas still in place, but they were originally intended to be used as jewelry.

BLISTERING BIVALVES

A dome-shaped pearl that has developed while attached to the inside surface of an oyster shell is known as a blister pearl. These are fairly common and are of little commercial value; they are generally used for decoration only. Very often the blisters reveal the nature of the object that is embedded against the shell, which may be a tiny crab or fish.

Freshwater pearls

PEARL OYSTER

Even small oysters can produce large pearls, although the older and larger the shell, the greater the chance of finding a good-sized pearl. This type of oyster grows to about 8 in (20 cm) and is common throughout the Indo-Pacific as well as the eastern Mediterranean, to which it made its way recently via the Suez Canal.

QUEEN MARY'S PEARLS

Before the advent of cultured pearls, jewelry made with natural pearls was extremely expensive and therefore a symbol of great wealth or status. Queen Mary of England is remembered for the long strings of pearls she wore.

Nacre, or
mother-of-pearl

Blue pearls

Black-lipped
oyster

White pearls

Detail from a 17th-century
French engraving,
Fishing for Pearls

PEARL FISHERS
Before aqualungs
became widely
available, pearl
divers had to be
extremely good
swimmers. In
Japan, women
known as *amas*
still dive down to
40 ft (12 m)
without air
tanks to collect
pearl oysters.
Making random
searches for oysters
that may contain
pearls is very
unproductive, since less
than one in a thousand
shells contains a good pearl.

Black pearls

**VARIETY
IN THE PEARL WORLD**
Pearls come in all shapes and
sizes: the largest in the world is
1½ in (3.8 cm) in diameter. The
shape of a pearl is also variable and,
while perfectly round pearls are the most
popular, some may be tear-shaped and others irregular.
Blue, black, and even yellow forms of pearl
exist and, because they are scarcer than the white forms,
they are more highly prized. The color depends on
the nature of the shell in which the pearls are formed
and the pigments secreted in the nacre.

PEARLY KINGS AND QUEENS
The traditional "holiday garments" worn by
East London street vendors consist of outfits
covered in pearl buttons. The custom goes back
to the Roman invasion of Britain, when
some British natives
wore shell costumes.

Pearl

DOG COCKLE PEARLS
Although not as attractive as
an oyster pearl, and therefore
less valuable, this pearl inside a
European dog cockle is a lot rarer.
Some pearls that come from shells
other than oysters may be very
valuable—the Caribbean conch shell, for
example, produces pink pearls, necklaces
of which can cost thousands of dollars.

Fossil finds

Fossilized
sand dollar
from Florida

WE ARE LUCKY IN THAT it is quite easy to trace the history of shelled animals back through many millions of years. The soft parts of an animal will rot away quickly after it dies, but the shells are preserved for long periods of time and can often be found as fossils (remains of the empty shell that have been turned into rock over millions of years, or identical casts of the long-gone shell). Fossil evidence shows how certain species have changed with the passage of time; in many cases animals have had to evolve in order to cope with changes in their environment, such as a change in temperature or in the sources of food available. Some animals have remained unchanged, presumably because they are in perfect harmony with their environment.

Tentacled
head would
have emerged
from here

Fossilized ammonites
from Dorset, England

Curled-up fossil trilobites

"Snakestone"
ammonite
forgery

FOSSIL FORGERY
Among the best-known fossils are those of the ammonites, which became extinct more than 65 million years ago. The ammonites were a form of cephalopod (p. 8) related to the nautilus still living today. In Whitby, England, the fossils were once thought to represent coiled serpents that had been beheaded and turned to stone by the Saxon abbess, St. Hilda. In order to maintain this legend, snakes' heads were commonly carved on fossil ammonites sold to tourists in the area.

Uncurled
trilobite

TALE OF THE TRILOBITES
The trilobites were another common animal that became extinct some 248 million years ago. These were primitive marine creatures related to the crustaceans that abound in our seas today. Like lobsters and crabs, trilobites had the ability to shed their plated skin, so trilobite fossils are fairly common. Some are found curled up, like a modern wood louse, for protection. There were thousands of species of trilobite—the largest type measuring some 28 in (70 cm) long.

Impression of trilobite
embedded in rock

Fossilized
lampshells

Fossil lampshells
embedded in rock

LAMPSHELLS
Belonging in a class
all their own, the
creatures known
as brachiopods, or
lampshells, were
once extremely
common. Their name comes from
their resemblance to certain types
of ancient oil lamp. Lampshells
resemble bivalve mollusks but
are unrelated. Fossil records
go back almost 600 million
years, and fossil lampshells are
sometimes found in large numbers.

Modern
brachiopod

Recent Neapolitan
triton shell

Fossilized Neapolitan
triton shell

**ALIVE AND WELL
AFTER 3 MILLION YEARS**
A creature that has been in
tune with its environment for
a long time, the Neapolitan triton
has hardly changed at all for 3 million
years. Although this is not very long in
geological terms, many similar types have
died out, implying that the Neapolitan
triton has truly found the secret to success.

BLOWING THE TRUMPET
Humans have inhabited
Earth for a very short time
compared to creatures with shells,
but we have used the empty shells in
various ways for thousands of years. Horns
made from conch and triton shells have been used to
signal over large distances by civilizations in all parts of the world.

Horseshoe crab
from below

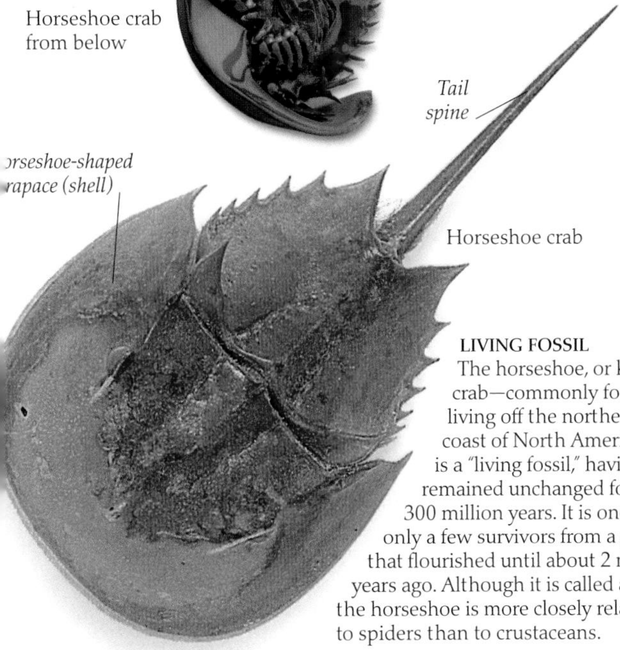

Tail
spine

Horseshoe-shaped
carapace (shell)

Horseshoe crab

PRESERVATION OF FOSSILS
The condition of a fossil depends mainly on its age and the type
of sediment in which it was deposited. Many fossils are solidly
embedded in hard rock; others exist in softer substances such as
clay. The fossil shells shown here were deposited only a couple
of million years ago, and
were found in soft soil
on a cliff only a little
way from the sea.
They are beautifully
preserved and as delicate
as modern shells.

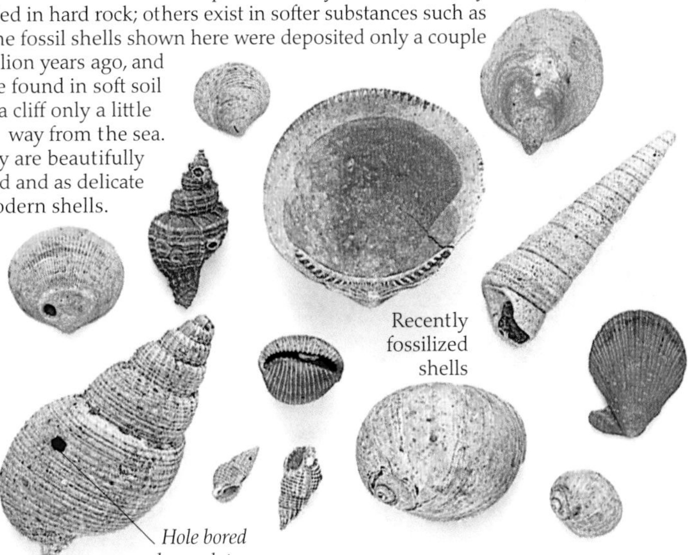

Recently
fossilized
shells

LIVING FOSSIL
The horseshoe, or king,
crab—commonly found
living off the northeast
coast of North America—
is a "living fossil," having
remained unchanged for
300 million years. It is one of
only a few survivors from a group
that flourished until about 2 million
years ago. Although it is called a crab, the
horseshoe is more closely related
to spiders than to crustaceans.

Hole bored
by predator

Cases for places

CHAMELEON SHRIMP
Cleverly concealed in a sea lettuce, this shrimp changes color to match the color of the seaweed on which it is living. At night, however, it always turns a transparent blue color.

IN THE WORLD OF NATURE, being seen or not seen can be the difference between life and death. As creatures move into new environments, or their environments change, those best suited are the ones that survive. They go through gradual changes, often over millions of years, that permit them to continue to live. Sometimes these are simply changes in habits; but in other cases, creatures evolve the art of camouflage—the ability to blend in with the background and stay unnoticed by predators in their chosen habitats. In the shell world, creatures have many ways of hiding themselves: there are crabs that cover themselves with algae, and mollusks that permanently secure loose objects to their shells.

Color also plays an important part in camouflage, and there are many shells that blend in perfectly with their surroundings. Some mollusks can actually change color almost instantly, like chameleons. Finally, there are some shells that simply allow themselves to be covered by plant growth, barnacles, or even deposits of lime.

Carrier shell with pebbles

Piece of glass bottle attached to carrier shell

Coral on which Babel's latiaxis lives

Latiaxis encrusted with marine growth

Underside of carrier shell and aperture (opening)

Aperture (opening) side of coated shell

Cleaned shell

WELCOME ATTACHMENTS
Although barnacles can be a nuisance when stuck to ships, they are useful as camouflage for the shore crab (above). If the crab keeps still, it looks more like a stone than a living creature.

SHELL COLLECTORS
Carrier shells get their name because as they grow, some of them attach a variety of objects to themselves, ranging from dead shells and coral to pebbles, and sometimes even pieces of garbage left by humans. They live mainly in deep water in most of the world's warm seas.

LIME COATINGS
When alive, most shells are crusted with marine algae and animals that make them difficult to find under water. Sometimes deposits can cover a shell entirely. Divers often have trouble locating latiaxis shells (left). They live on coral, and are often so well disguised that the divers have to feel along the coral surface for the shells with their hands.

Snail in the grass

The color diversity within land snail shells often seems infinite. The common European banded snail displays enormous variety in its shell color and pattern, each blending it in with its habitat and protecting it from predators.

DECIDUOUS WOODLAND
Brownish-colored shells without any banding are more likely to go unnoticed by birds and other predators in deciduous (leaf-shedding) woodland areas. The snails often hide among leaf litter on the forest floor.

LONG GRASS
Snails with yellow banded shells usually live on strands of long grass and manage to go unnoticed by predators.

SHORT TURF
From the air, short grass is fairly uniform in color, and the yellow unbanded shells of snails that live among the turf are the least noticeable.

BEECH LITTER
Heavily banded shells are common among the leaf litter in a beech forest. The banding density varies according to the type of litter in which the shells live.

Settlers on the sands

UNLIKE A ROCKY COASTLINE or coral reef (pp. 46–53), a sandy shore seems to offer little shelter for shelled creatures. However, in order to avoid being exposed, many of the animals found on sandy shores are burrowers, sometimes spending their entire lives buried deep below the surface. When a sandy beach is exposed at low tide it seems a lifeless, apparently barren environment, but close inspection will reveal a variety of holes, mounds, and tracks—all evidence of animals that have dug down to where moisture is retained until the next tide. Sometimes hundreds of shells may be living in an area of sand no larger than this page.

Necklace shells

FLAT-SIDE UP
Scallops are a popular food (p. 35), and the scallop shell is the symbol of Saint James, the fisherman. The two valves of Saint James's scallop are very different in shape: the bottom valve is domed and the top valve is flattened. The scallops lie with their bottom valve buried in the sand.

Saint James's scallop

NECKLACE SHELLS
Necklace shells get their names because they lay their eggs in coiled, straplike bands. These gastropod mollusks are common predators that plow through the sand in search of food. They drill circular holes in bivalve shells and eat the animals inside.

SUNDIAL SHELLS
These gastropods, also known as architect shells, have elegant spiral patterns and are found on tropical sandy shores. Some sundial shells measure just a fraction of an inch in diameter and live in very deep water.

Tropical sundials

SANDY EXPANSES
The long stretches of sandy beach that occur on many coasts are formed by waves, tides, and currents. Sea cliffs are eroded by waves and weather, and the rock, mixed with shells, is broken into tiny particles. This mixture eventually ends up as sand; onshore as a beach, and offshore as a sandbar or sandbank.

MARGIN SHELLS
These colorful shells can be found on the sandy shores of many warm countries. Empty specimens that wash up on the beach do not usually have the naturally polished look of living shells.

SPOTTED DIGGERS
These colorful acteon shells burrow into the sand with their flattened, spadelike heads. Acteon shells can be found in many of the world's seas; these two are of a type discovered in the Persian Gulf.

Eloise's acteon

West African margin shells

BURROWING BIVALVES
The majority of shells found on sandy shores are bivalves. The Mediterranean scraper solecurtus and the Indo-Pacific sunset siliqua (both also known as razor clams) are typical of bivalve shells that use their muscles to pull themselves deep into the sand when the tide goes out.

BUBBLES AND CANOES
Canoe bubble shells are mollusks that occur in a variety of marine environments. They slide along the surface of fine mud in search of small mollusks, which they eat by crushing them with their powerful gizzards (stomachs). The animals are often many times larger than their fragile, inflated shells.

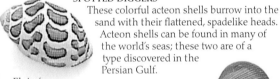

Canoe bubble shell

Sunset siliqua

Scraper solecurtus

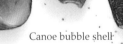

Razor shell

Junonia
volute

KEEPING A TOEHOLD
The oddly shaped pelican's foot
shell lives on muddy gravel
below the low-tide
mark. Its shelly "toes"
seem to serve as an
anchorage in this
soft base. These
common shells
were widely collected
in the 19th century
for use in shell art.

Pelican's
foot shell

BORING SHELL
This marlinspike shell is the
largest of a group of shells
called augers—named after a
tool used for boring into wood.
These long and slender shells are
found mainly on tropical beaches
and are perfectly adapted
for digging in the sand.

Marlinspike
auger

Worm tube
made from sand

**THE
JUNONIA**
This volute
shell (p. 13)
lives in
sand off the
southeastern United
States. A large and
colorful shell, it is
highly prized by
shell collectors.

**TUSKLIKE
TUBES**
These "shells"
resemble those of tusk shells (p. 18)
but are in fact tubes of sand sculpted
by certain marine worms. The grains
of sand are bound together by
mucous secreted by the worm, and
the tubes lie buried in the
sand, with only the worm's
tentacled head appearing
above the surface.

INDIAN SCREW SHELL
The multiwhorled
turritella, or screw shell,
burrows into muddy gravel by
moving jerkily from side to side,
using its shell as a digging tool.

SPINDLE SHELL
The high-spired spindle shell is another
sand-burrowing predatory mollusk. These
shells occur in most of the world's warmer seas,
some tropical
types reaching
lengths of over
8 in (20 cm).

The marlinspike
auger can
grow 6–8 in
(15–20 cm) long

Indian
turritella

East African
spindle shell

SHARP MOVER
haped like old-style "cut-throat"
zors, and often nearly as sharp, these
valve mollusks can burrow deep into
e sand very rapidly, using their wedge-
aped foot to pull the shell downward.
he two razor shell valves are joined by
strong ligament, and the valves of dead
imals can often be found still attached
each other.

Exhalant
siphon

Inhalant
siphon

Hairs on
antennae
interlock to form
breathing tube

LIFE DOWN UNDER
The burrowing mollusks breathe and feed
through long extensions called siphons.
Each lives at its own depth,
some near the surface,
others deep down, and
their siphons may be
extremely long. The overall
length of some bivalve
mollusks can be 4–5 times
that of their shells. Some
crustaceans also live below
the sand; the masked crab
digs down with its legs so
that only the tips of its long
antennae stick out above
the surface during the day.
It only appears at night
to forage for food.

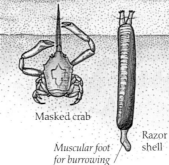

Masked crab

Razor
shell

Muscular foot
for burrowing

Sand
gaper

Tusk
shell

Tellin

Male
masked
crab

COVERING CLAWS
The Calappa crab buries itself
in the sand using its claws.
Some say that it throws sand
over itself rather than burrow.

Calappa crab

Female
masked crab

Pelican's foot
shell

Foliate tellin

Razor shell

Continued on next page

PREYING MANTIS

The large mantis shrimp is not likely to be found on the beach because it usually lives below tidal levels. Its thin, light shell allows it to move quickly along the seabed in pursuit of prey, which it crushes with its front legs. In parts of the Mediterranean, this shrimp is fished commercially for food.

Spiny crushers

Mantis shrimp

SINGLE-CELLED ANIMALS

Looking at sand through a microscope reveals the shells of many types of marine creature. Among the most common are the strangely shaped single-celled creatures known as foraminifera, or forams which live at all depths of the oceans. Some areas of the seafloor are made up of millions upon millions of these tiny shells.

Stichostega

Helixostega

Entomostega

MINIATURE MOLLUSKS

Mollusk shells come in all shapes and sizes. Sometimes sand is made up almost entirely of small shells and shell fragments. Perfectly formed miniatures of the snail shells shown on the previous pages can be found among the sand on many beaches

SMALL FRY

Shrimp occur in many types of marine environment, often in great numbers. When disturbed, they are able to shoot backward with a swift movement of their tail fans. Shrimp use their legs and long feelers to bury themselves in the sand, with just the shorter pair of antennae poking out to detect nearby prey.

Antennae

Shrimp

Walking legs

Langoustine

Tail fan

Dark blotches to discourage predators attacking from behind

Paddlelike limbs for swimming

THE STORY OF SAND

There are many different types of sand, but all of them are by-products of weathering and erosion by the waves. Near stony coral reefs in the tropics, parrotfish droppings, containing broken-down coral skeletons they have eaten, add to the sand. Rock particles, broken shells, parrot fish droppings, fish skeletons, glass, and pieces of coral are all deposited onto beaches and continually worn down to tiny grains by wave movement.

GIANT SANDMAN

The sand that makes up deserts on dry land is often formed through the wind erosion of rocks. Some desert sand, however, was formed by water erosion and deposited by the oceans many millions of years ago. The Sphinx and the great pyramids of Egypt are all built from sandstone, which contains the fossilized shells of billions of minute marine creatures known as nummulites.

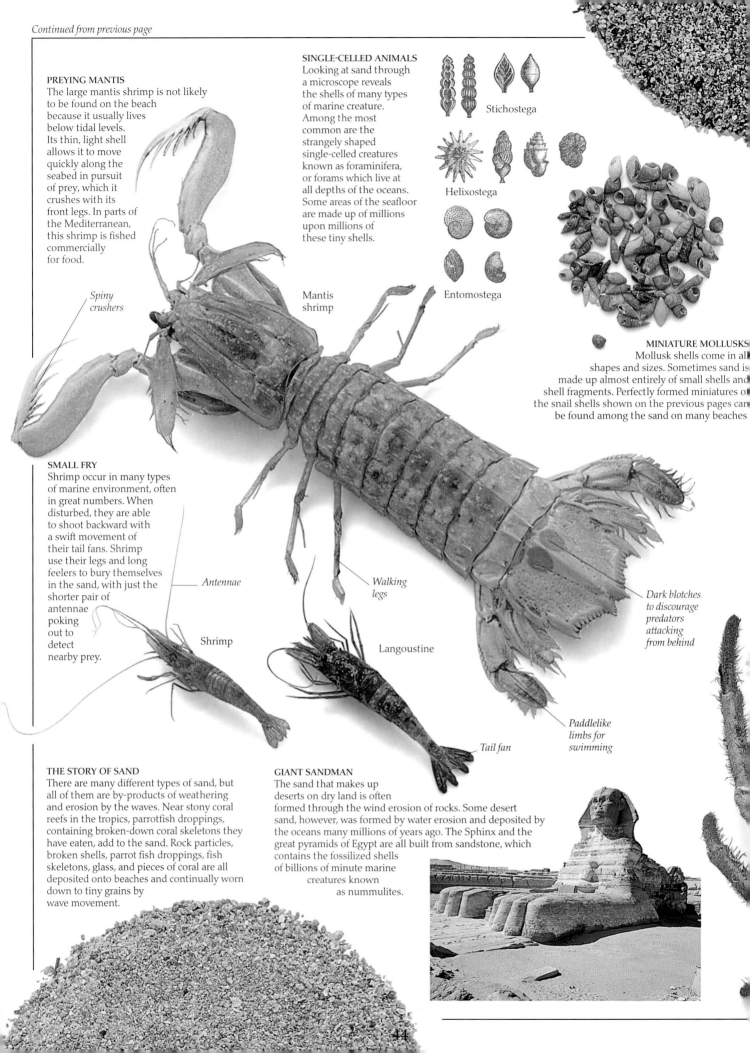

Sand made up
of small shells and
tiny shell fragments

Spines

Sand dollar
with spines

Swimming crab

SWIMMING CRAB
Some of the crabs living on
sandy shores have adapted
their fifth pair of legs for
swimming rather than
walking, the last joint
being shaped like a
rounded, flat paddle.

*Swimming
paddles*

Caribbean
sea biscuit

Philippine
sand dollar

*Long pincer for
catching prey in
deep crevices*

Spiny spider crab

*Barnacles and
worm tubes
attached to
carapace*

Walking legs

**STAYING
POWER**
Sea urchins, which
include sand dollars and
sea biscuits, are typical inhabitants
of sandy shores in warmer areas,
especially Caribbean and Australian
waters. The living sand dollar is covered
in hundreds of tiny spines and lives
just below the surface of the sand.
Its flattened shape permits the
sand dollar to stay in the same spot
as water flows smoothly over it.

THORNS IN THE SAND
The spiny spider crab (p. 25) is
easily recognizable by its small,
spiny body and long legs. Its
carapace (shell) is often encrusted
with other marine organisms, and
young crabs are known to cover themselves
with seaweed and algae for camouflage. They
live on the lower shore and gather to breed in
the summer, forming heaps of up to 80 crabs.
Because of their spiny carapaces, these crabs
are also known as thornbacks. Fishermen
searching for thornbacks submerged in
the sand walk the beaches barefoot
and feel for the crabs with their feet.

Life on the rocks

ROCKY SHORES provide a diverse and complex environment for many types of marine creature. The types of rock from which a beach is made, its position in relation to the sea, and the range of tide levels all play a part in determining the variety of creatures that live there. Where the tide exposes the rocky shore for several hours each day, some creatures have built up a tolerance to living without water for extended periods. Those that have not managed to reach deeper waters or find tidal pools when the water recedes, will dry out and die from exposure to air and sunlight. These are not the only elements to which a rocky shore may be exposed; the pounding of powerful waves erodes the rocks themselves. Many animals living on the rocks have evolved very strong shells that can withstand the force of the waves, and many have developed ways of anchoring themselves firmly to the surface of the rocks, so they are not washed away. The rocky seabed plays host to an even wider range of creatures, many of which spend much of their lives hidden in holes or underneath rocks.

ROCK-POOL INHABITANTS
Life can be hard in the shallow pools left by receding tides. Many creatures that prefer less light and warmth are left stranded and must try their best to find shelter in this extreme environment.

Bearded ark shell

BEARDED ARK SHELL
So called because of the tiny hairs that cover its shell, this is a bivalve that lives in rock crevices, attaching itself by means of a broad byssus (see below). The shell of this creature is often distorted as it grows to fit snugly in its rocky recess.

New Zealand mussel

Mussel with byssal threads

Common blue mussels

Tail fan

MUSSELS WITH ANCHORS
Mussels are common inhabitants of many rocky coasts, often living in massive clusters high on the shore. Mussels anchor themselves to rocks and other surfaces by means of byssal threads—strong, thin filaments planted by the mussel's foot.

THE JEWEL IN THE SHELL
This rough star shell lives on the rocky shores of the Mediterranean, but is found below tide level. The shell is often heavily encrusted with marine growths. The bright-red operculum is sometimes used to make jewelry.

Operculum

WINKLES ON THE WEEDS
The tiny periwinkles are among the most common inhabitants of rocky shores. These snails live high up on the shore, clinging to rocks and clumps of seaweed.

Rough periwinkles

Antenna

Claw

Common shore crab

COMMON CRAB
The shore crab is one of the most common European crabs and can be found lurking under rocks and seaweed.

STONY-SHELLED CRAB
The Mediterranean stone crab is named for its heavy-looking, irregular shell.

ELUSIVE LOBSTER
The common lobster is highly prized for food and is a favorite catch for divers. Lobsters can be difficult to find, as they blend in with their surroundings and often hide away in crevices during the day, with only their claws and antennae showing.

Walking legs

COLORFUL EAR SHELLS
Abalones, or ormers, like this California green abalone, are also known as ear shells because of their shape. The row of holes in the shell allows water and waste to be passed out. The animals inside are eaten in many parts of the world, and the shells are used to make jewelry.

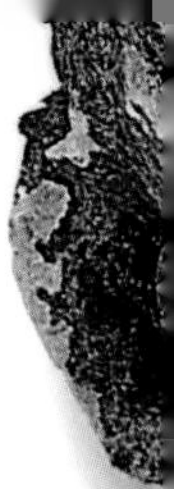

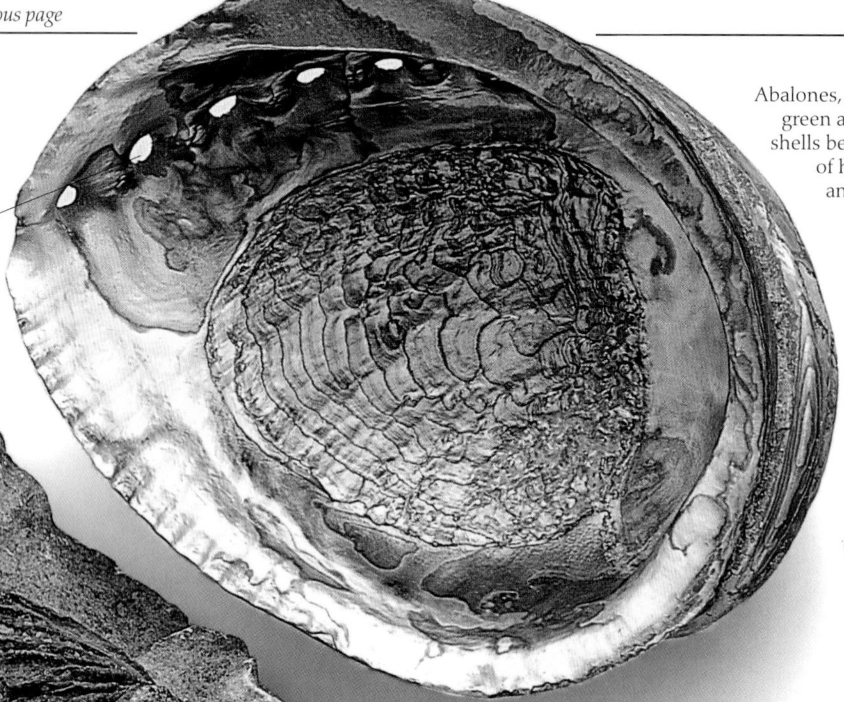

Holes for expulsion of water and waste

Green abalone

Chiton shell (p. 18)

BARNACLE ROCK SHELL
This odd-looking shell, found off the coasts of Peru and Chile, is related to the murex shells (p. 12), but it sits on rocks, much like a limpet (below).

LONG-LASTING LIMPETS
Limpets are known for holding on tightly to rocks so as not to be knocked off by strong waves. A magnetic mine that clings to ships' hulls is named after them. Limpet shells are usually either very eroded or covered with algae and other forms of marine life.

Barnacles and algae on limpet shell

Safian limpet shell

KILLER SNAILS
Most rocky shores play host to snails that feed on bivalves such as mussels and oysters. Some "drill" into the shells of their prey; others, such as the Panamanian thorn latirus, have developed a special tooth that helps to break open the shells. The Sting winkle is another example of a predatory sea snail.

Thorn latirus

Tooth

Sting winkle

European china limpet

Rock-boring shells

Some shelled creatures have overcome the problem of being washed away by strong waves by sticking to rocks permanently, or even boring into them. These animals feed by extending tubes or fans out from their shells to catch prey, or by opening their valves and allowing the current to bring microscopic food to them. The creatures that hide away in holes in the rocks are not only safe from being washed away, but are also protected from most of their enemies.

Limestone

Shell

Top valve of shell

Calcareous tube

BURROWING SEA URCHINS
Certain types of sea urchin use their spines to dig out holes in sand, mud, or rocks. This protects them from the force of waves or currents. They hold on to the rock with their rows of suckered tube feet.

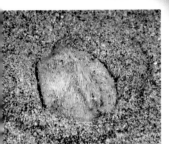

READY-MADE HOMES
Retzius shells settle in holes that already exist in rocks, but the animal enlarges its home as it grows. Eventually, it becomes firmly wedged in, making it impossible for the shell to be dislodged by the waves.

GIVE-AWAY TUBE
Some of the creatures that live inside rocks are only visible because of a shelly tube, which they extend from their hidden home.

STUCK LIKE GLUE
The jewel-box shell is a bivalve that does not live inside the rock but cements its lower valve to the surface in the same way as some types of oyster.

DIGGING DOWN DEEP
The piddock shell can be found buried in a variety of hard substances, which it bores into mechanically with its two valves. Some types of piddock can live up to 3 ft (1 m) below the surface.

Piddock hole in rock

Piddock shell and siphon

Date mussel removed from rock

Shell embedded in rock

Piddock shell removed from rock

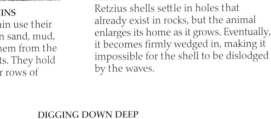

ROCK EROSION
Unlike the piddock, date mussels do not use their valves to bore holes. Instead, they secrete a special chemical that softens the rock. Then the rock is scraped away and flushed out by water currents from the mussel's siphons. Date mussels are edible.

SHELLS UPON SHELLS
Shells that spend their lives stuck to one spot frequently provide suitable homes for other shells. White shelly tubes belonging to a certain type of marine worm are often seen on rocks and other shells.

Worm tubes on thorny oyster

BLISTERING BARNACLES
Barnacles often cling to rocky shorelines in massive colonies. They also attach themselves to the undersides of boats and have to be scraped off so they don't slow the boat down.

WHERE'S THE WORM?
Although commonly called worm shells, these irregularly shaped tubes belong to gastropod mollusks, which spend their lives cemented to hard surfaces.

Cluster of barnacles

Worm shells on rock

Worm tubes on Mediterranean blue mussel shell

Residents of the reefs

C ORAL REEFS ARE COMPLEX NETWORKS
of millions of living organisms, supporting
more life than any other type of marine
environment. They are like underwater
gardens, with a wide variety of different
colors and textures, and very dependent on sunlight
and warmth for survival. Most coral occurs in warm
regions of the world; many large coral outcrops are found in
the Caribbean, off West Africa, and throughout the Indo-Pacific.
Some outcrops are huge, the most famous being Australia's Great
Barrier Reef, which stretches for more than 1,250 miles (2,000 km).
Among the multitude of animals inhabiting the reefs are many
shelled creatures, although they may be difficult to spot because
they hide under or between the corals during the day. Not until
the relative safety of darkness do they emerge in search of food.
The shallow-water reefs and the life they support are extremely
vulnerable, and although many coral reefs were established
long before humans existed on
Earth, they are being threatened
by pollution, global warming,
and over-eager collectors.

**LEGENDS
OF THE REEFS**
Mermaids and
sea nymphs
are legendary
creatures thought
by ancient sailors
to inhabit the seas
around coral reefs.
They are often
shown as using
the spiny shell
of a murex to
comb their
long hair.

Violet
coral shell

VIOLET CORAL SHELL
These little shells are typical
inhabitants of tropical reefs,
usually living in the crevices
or hollows of live coral heads.
Females of this species are
often larger than males.

Princely
cone

Marble
cone

*Fluted
growth layers*

**FLUTED
FILTER FEEDER**
A smaller relative of the
giant clam (p. 17), which grows to more
than 5 ft (1.5 m) in length, this pretty clam
can be found on shallow reefs throughout
most of the Indo-Pacific area. It is a filter
feeder—it lies with its valves apart and sifts
tiny plants and animals from the water.

Papal miter

CONES AND MITERS
Some of the largest and most decorative
mollusk shells of the coral reefs are the
cone and miter shells. Although they
belong to different families, both
shells are prized for their
bright colors and patterns.
Cone shells (p. 12) are also
famous for their ability to
shoot a paralyzing dart into
their prey. This has killed
some shell collectors.

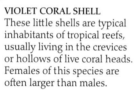

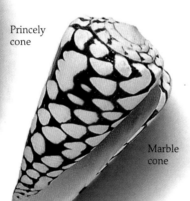

COLORFUL COWRIES
Among the
prettiest and
most diverse
creatures to be
found on the reefs
are the popular
cowrie shells. The
smaller types often
live on the underside
of coral slabs.

Blue coral

Oldest whorls of shell

Scorpion murex

Brachiopod

Jewel-box shells

SECURE SUPPORT
Cemented firmly in place, jewel-box shells and a brachiopod form a micro-community on this piece of Atlantic coral.

BURROWING CORAL SHELLS
One of the most unusual shells inhabiting the reef is the burrowing coral shell, which spends its life deeply embedded in brain coral. As the mollusk grows, it slowly builds a long, irregular tube and fills the oldest whorls with shelly matter.

Map cowrie

Mole cowrie

Zambo's murex

ADAPTING TO LIFE ON THE REEF
Many of the murex shells that live around the reefs are shaped as if to mimic the coral itself. The living shells are often heavily encrusted with marine growth, which provides excellent camouflage. The scorpio conch also has distinctive spines that enable it to crawl on the sand around the reef without being swept away by strong underwater currents.

Scorpio conch

COLLECTORS' PIECES
The obvious beauty and relative ease with which most cowries can be found on a shallow-water reef make them targets for shell collectors. Unfortunately, too much collecting on the more easily reached reefs in the Pacific has threatened many once-thriving populations. The demand for these shells has encouraged collecting as a full-time occupation in some areas of the tropics.

Eyed cowrie

Turtle cowrie

COLORLESS CORAL CORPSE
The "coral" that many people recognize is usually just a bleached, white skeleton of what was once a massive community of tiny, brightly colored creatures known as polyps. Coral comes in all shapes and sizes, and shells can often be found hidden underneath or within the fragile structure of both living and dead coral. Although all corals can be decorative, it is usually the deep-water forms that are fished for use in jewelry.

51

Continued on next page

BORN OF THE OCEAN
Rising out of the sea, Erskine Island off Queensland, Australia, is made from dead coral and surrounded by living coral. Thousands of tiny coral islands such as this one can be found on Australia's Great Barrier Reef.

TROPICAL TURTLES
Marine turtles can sometimes be seen in the warm waters surrounding tropical coral reefs. The hawksbill turtle (p. 31) is a typical coral-reef dweller. Because of the abundance of marine life, shallow-water reefs are ideal feeding grounds for many types of creature. Some marine turtles have developed incredible migratory habits, traveling hundreds of miles from their feeding grounds to nest on the beaches where they were born. The green turtle (below) travels to its nesting ground every two or three years.

Green turtle

Color range in tests of tropical sea urchins

SPINY REEF-DWELLERS
Common inhabitants of most coral reefs are the sea urchins (p. 20). Their spine-covered tests are usually found in reef hollows. Sea urchins are mainly herbivorous (plant-eating), feeding on tiny algae scraped off rock and dead coral.

CARNIVOROUS PLANT?
This strange-looking specimen may look like a plant, but it is in fact polyps. This straw tubularia is a carnivorous (eats zooplankton) polyp with long stems encased in yellowish tubes. These creatures attach themselves readily to shells and stones.

Smooth laminae (bony plates) do not overlap

Color of shell can be green, brown, or black

Skeleton of
brain coral

BRAIN OR MUSHROOM?
Two of the most common types of coral found in tropical areas are brain corals and mushroom corals. From the pictures, it is not difficult to see where they got their names! Brain corals, made by a colony containing millions of tiny coral polyps, grow into a heap with patterning like the folds found on brains. The smaller mushroom corals are disklike, look almost edible, and, because they are not attached to a hard base, can move short distances.

Skeleton of
mushroom coral

Living brain
coral in front
of sea fan

Crustaceans and corals

The crustaceans have successfully made homes for themselves in coral reefs, as they have in all marine environments. Crabs, lobsters, and shrimp can be found there in great variety. Some, such as the coral-gall crab (below), actually live inside the coral; others display bright colors or unusual shapes that help them to blend in with the coral garden.

CORAL-DWELLING CRAB
The coral-gall crab settles on coral when very young and becomes enveloped as the coral grows.

A LIVING PEARL
With its knobby shell, the tropical spotted rock crab, or pearl crab (below), is easily recognizable.

Galls on the living coral

NOW YOU SEE IT...
The ghost crab is so called because it is the same color as the sandy tropical beaches where it lives, and it seems to appear and disappear at random.

Deep-sea dwellers

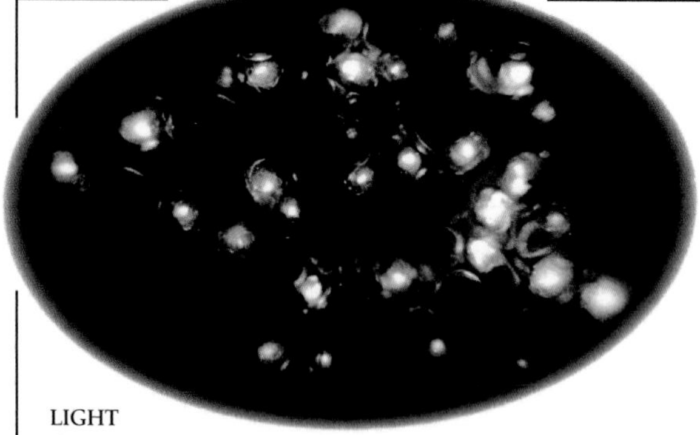

LIGHT OF THE DEPTHS
Many deep-sea creatures have evolved methods that make them glow. This light, known as bioluminescence, is seen above in tiny crustaceans called ostracods.

A SURPRISING AMOUNT OF EARTH'S SURFACE—about 70 percent—is under water, covered by the oceans. The sea plunges to great depths off the world's land masses—in some areas to over 33,500 ft (10,200 m). With this huge amount of water, it is little wonder that the ocean depths are among the least known, most mysterious areas of our planet. By contrast with the seabed near the coast, which is covered with rocks and jungles of seaweed, the floor of the deep sea is barren, covered with a kind of soft, gray ooze. Deep-sea explorers and fishermen are constantly dredging up previously unknown types of sea creature. Most of the deep-sea shelled creatures are mollusks, crustaceans, and echinoderms—groups that we know from more shallow coastal waters. Almost everything that dies in the oceans eventually drifts down to the seabed to form matter known as detritus, and most deep-sea creatures feed by taking nutrients from this.

Victor Dan's delphinula (Philippines)

Hirase's slit shell (Japan)

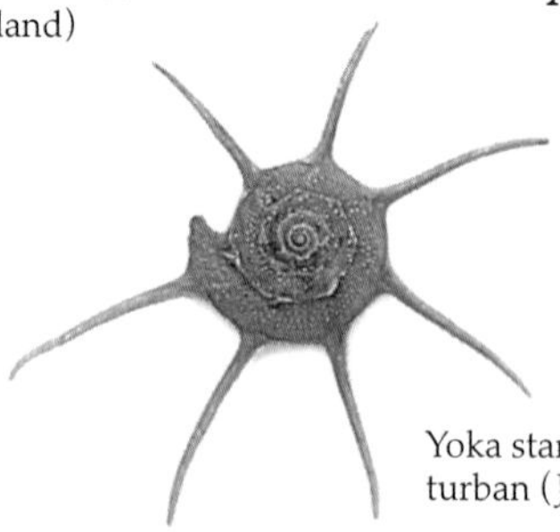

Sunburst star turban (New Zealand)

Yoka star turban (Japan)

Margarite shell (Taiwan)

Deep-sea gastropods
Shells found in deep water, where there is no light, tend to be less colorful than those, for instance, from coral reefs. However, there is no shortage of beauty or variety among deep-sea gastropods. Most of the examples above were once thought to be extremely rare, but as fishing techniques improve, more and more specimens are being found. The delphinula shell (top left) was discovered in the Philippines.

UNDERWATER LAMPS
The transparent, glassy lampshells (right) are not brightly colored, which is typical of many deep-sea dwellers. Some 300 different types of lampshell exist, and many of them live in deep water. They attach themselves to solid bases by using a muscular stalk.

Mediterranean lampshells

Deep-sea crustacea

Crustaceans are among the most abundant of creatures to be found in deep water. They range from tiny ostracods (see opposite) to massive crabs, like the Japanese spider crab (leg shown below), and blind deep-sea lobsters whose fossils were known long before living examples were found. Some of the larger crustaceans are fished by laying traps, but most of them live a peaceful life in the darkness of the seabed, out of human reach.

CRAB ON THE SEABED
The square, or angular, crab can be found in the Mediterranean and northeast Atlantic seas, at depths to 500 ft (150 m). It lives in burrows on the seabed.

Angular crab

Japanese spider crab leg shown at half its actual size

DADDY LONGLEGS
The largest of all crustaceans is the giant Japanese spider crab. With its long claws outstretched, it can span 12 ft (3.7 m) and its carapace can measure 18 in (46 cm) across. Fishermen, famous for exaggerating, have claimed that crabs 300 ft (92 m) across exist. Found in the North Pacific off Japan, the fearsome-looking spider crab is caught for food and no doubt provides enough to feed a large family.

Rathbun's giant lima, or file shell (Philippines)

MONSTER FROM THE DEPTHS
These pictures from the *Japan Diaries* of 19th-century naturalist Richard Gordon Smith show the incredible proportions of the spider crab. The man wearing the carapace on his head is dwarfed by the crab's enormous claws. The Japanese watercolor below shows the "monster" chasing children up a beach.

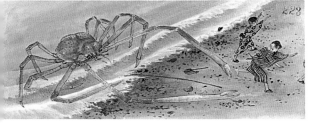

Deep-sea bivalves

The soft ooze that covers the base rock on most of the oceans' floors is ideally suited to burrowing bivalve mollusks. These filter feeders get their food from the organic materials that drift down from the sea above. Deep-sea submarines have discovered giant bivalves on the seabed at depths of 1.5 miles (2.5 km). The giant file shell (above) was dredged by a Russian research ship at a depth of 1,180 ft (360 m).

Freshwater finds

THE VARIETY OF LIFE in freshwater habitats, such as rivers and estuaries, is not as great as in the world's seas. All freshwater creatures began life in the sea and developed from marine creatures millions of years ago. Many belong to the same families that live today in marine environments. The freshwater crustaceans, mollusks, and turtles all have bodies that have successfully adapted to life in freshwater. Their habits have adapted, too, enabling them to go upstream from the seas and maintain their ground against the constant flow of water and strong currents. Many freshwater creatures lay eggs that can be secured to plants, or give birth to live young—the free-swimming larvae common to many sea creatures would have no chance of survival and would be washed away downstream toward the sea.

A CRAB WITH MITTENS
Some types of crab live both in freshwater and in brackish water environments, such as estuaries and mangrove swamps. The Chinese mitten crab, or woolly handed crab (above) lives in estuaries in Asia. It has been introduced in the Europe and North America, where it is considered a pest. With its characteristic furry cuff, it is easy to see how it got its name.

FRESHWATER LOBSTER
Crayfish live in freshwater habitats in many parts of the world—in Louisiana, they are a staple of Cajun cooking. They tend to live under stones or in shallow burrows. Most crayfish will lie low until a small fish or some other tempting morsel passes by, and then will snap it up in their powerful claws. Not all crayfish are active the whole year round: some dig deep burrows in which they remain all winter; others swim out to deeper waters and lie on the bottom until the weather warms again.

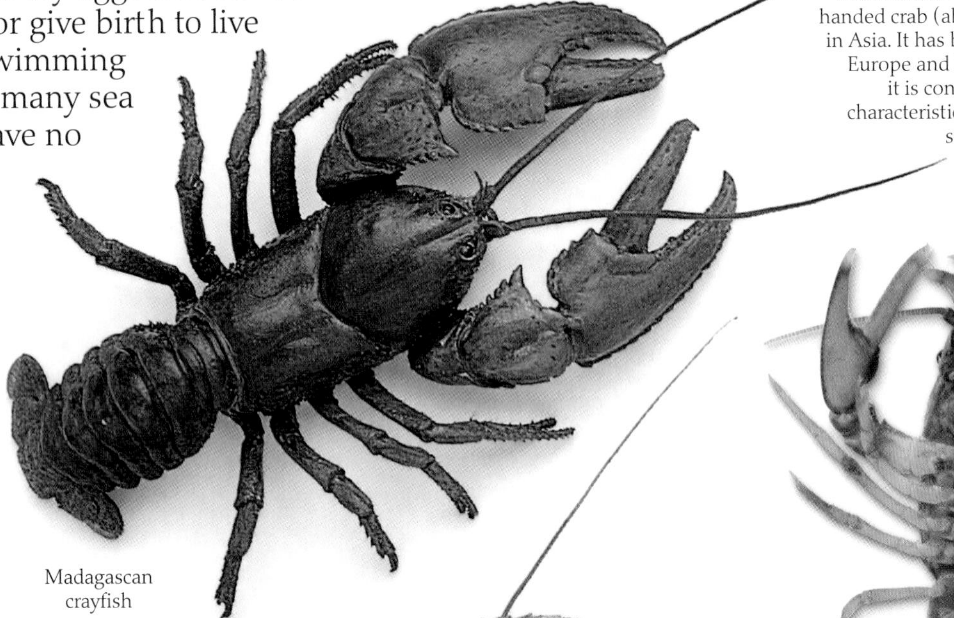

Madagascan crayfish

Underside of a crayfish

Murray River crayfish

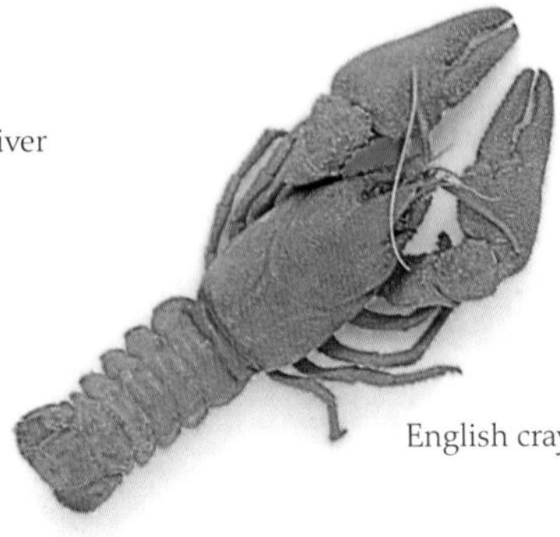

English crayfish

ON THE HUNT

Turtles are found both in marine and freshwater habitats. The European pond turtle is one of over 80 species of mainly freshwater turtle living today. A meat-eating turtle, it hunts both in the water and on land, feeding on small fish, worms, mollusks, and frogs.

European pond turtle

A REAL SOFTIE

Most members of the tortoise family have hardened carapaces, but the spiny soft-shelled river turtle from North America has a rounded, flexible carapace with no bony plates at all. Unlike other members of its family, the soft-shell is able to move fast both in water and on land.

SNAPPING, NOT NAPPING

The alligator snapping turtle is one of the most bizarre-looking of all the turtles. It catches prey by lying totally still on the riverbed, with its huge mouth agape. Within its mouth is a fleshy, pink appendage that looks like a wriggling worm. Any unsuspecting fish that takes this "bait" finds instant death between the turtle's powerful, snapping jaws. The alligator snapping turtle inhabits deep rivers and lakes of central North America, where it is often caught for food.

Alligator snapping turtle

South American ram's-horn snails

Giant Amazonian river snail

Giant Venezuelan river snail

African apple snail

FRESHWATER MOLLUSKS

Mollusks living in freshwater environments tend to have lighter, thinner shells than marine ones and are less colorful, enabling them to blend in well with their surroundings. Freshwater gastropods come in all shapes and sizes, the largest ones being the river snails of the South American Amazon and freshwater snails of Africa, such as the apple snail. Gastropods and bivalves are the only types of mollusk that live in freshwater.

Inland inhabitants

MOST TYPES OF SHELLED CREATURE make their homes in the world's oceans. But there are some that have emerged slowly from the sea over millions of years and evolved to live on land. Among the most successful of these creatures are the mollusks, including many thousands of different types of land snail that live in environments as diverse as deserts and tropical rain forests. Some live high up in the branches of the forest canopy; others can be found several feet under ground. A few crustaceans have adapted successfully to the land. Reptiles first appeared on land, and while most of the shelled forms have returned to water, one family, the tortoises, stay on dried land.

Coconut husk broken by robber crab

Powerful claws

Strengthened carapace

CRABS IN THE TREES

The robber, or "coconut," crab can be found on some Pacific islands. A tree-climbing giant, it can grow up to 18 in (45 cm) long and climbs trees in search of coconuts, which it cracks open with its powerful claws. As a young adult, the crab carries a mollusk shell, like a hermit crab, and when it has outgrown this, it carries half a coconut! Eventually, it relies on its claws and hardened exoskeleton for protection. On some islands, the crab is hunted for food. When caught, however, the robber crab must be held carefully to avoid serious injury, as this Cook Islander (left) is demonstrating.

Common
woodlouse

ARMORED LOUSE
Of all the crustaceans, the most
completely adapted to life on
land are the woodlice. They can
be found in every garden,
under stones or flower pots.
Woodlice gather in damp or
humid spots, feeding on
decaying vegetable matter and,
of course, rotting wood.

*Starry pattern
on carapace
laminae*

STARRY SHELL
Unlike their relatives the
turtles and terrapins, most
tortoises live on land. Like
these aquatic cousins, tortoises
carry a shell or carapace on top of
their bodies. Made from bony plates
known as laminae, a tortoise's shell
often displays quite beautiful
patterns. This starred tortoise,
from India and Sri Lanka, is so
called because of the striking
geometric patterns on its
carapace, very much like little
black and yellow stars.

Tree bark

*Sharply pointed
feet help robber
crab to climb*

A Japanese
tortoise
charmer—
safer than
snakes!

A snail emerges

Not famed for their mobility or
speed, land snails are, in fact, quite
clever when they need to be. These
photographs illustrate how a snail
uses its strong muscles to right its shell.

A sudden jerk
of the mollusk
corrects the shell's
position.

Its foot fully
extended, the
snail steams
off at full speed.

Removed from
its resting place,
the mollusk hides
within its shell to
protect its soft body.

The snail's
foot begins to
emerge tentatively,
taking in its new
surroundings.

As the foot
emerges, the changing
distribution of weight
rocks the shell over.

The entire foot of the
snail is now out and
the head is directed
under the shell.

Shells in strange places

IN THE CONSTANT STRUGGLE FOR SURVIVAL, plants and animals
have evolved to occupy a great variety of land, freshwater, and marine
environments. In the world of shelled creatures, there are many
peculiar habitats that are occupied by only one type of shelled animal.
Many of these animals have learned that the best way to survive is
not to be too fussy—barnacles and some types of worm are concerned
only with having a solid base on which to live. Some animals have
developed close associations with other creatures and, in fact, live
off them; others will cling
to almost any secure
surface they can find.

*Brachiopod,
or lampshell*

**LINGERING
LAMPSHELL**
Brachiopods, or lampshells,
attach themselves to solid
surfaces by means of a flexible
stalk and can sometimes
be found living on mollusk
shells, as here.

Barnacles

COCKLE COLONY
Covering this
empty cockle shell
are hundreds of white
shelly tubes made
by a type of marine
worm. These worms
attach themselves to
almost any solid
surface available and
often live in large
colonies. They extend
their tentacles from
the end of the tubes
to catch particles of
food that float past.

*Calcareous
worm tubes*

Mollusk

Worm tube
on a top shell

Mollusk shell

IN A SPIN
As if wanting
to imitate its
shelled partner, this worm
tube has slowly followed
the spiral coiling of the
mollusk on which it sits.

MIXED MOLLUSKS
This thorny oyster,
a bivalve mollusk,
has two very
different types
of marine animal
attached to its
shell. Although the
white shelly tubes
are all worm-shaped,
the largest one
actually belongs to a
gastropod mollusk.

*Worm
tubes*

Goose barnacles

A WHOLE HOST OF VISITORS
Submerged under water for about 2,000 years,
this Roman two-handled jar (right) has probably
played host to thousands of different marine
creatures. There are three distinct types visible
here: barnacles, worm tubes, and mollusks.

SHELLY SHIPWRECKERS

Much as termites will eat through wood on land, teredo shipworms will do equal damage to lumber in the sea, and have long been the scourge of wooden shipbuilders. Although called a shipworm, it is actually a bivalve mollusk that makes the holes and the shelly tubes they contain. The mollusk's tiny shell is used more as a drilling tool than for protection.

Holes made by shipworms

Shipworms often had a devastating effect on early sailing ships

Shelly tubes of shipworm removed from wood

Helmet shell

HIDEAWAY HERMIT
The hermit crab (right), often seen in shallow water pools, is not the natural inhabitant of the shell in which it lives. This crab (p. 33) does not possess a hard shell of its own, so it "borrows" an empty mollusk shell and as it grows discards its home in favor of a more spacious one.

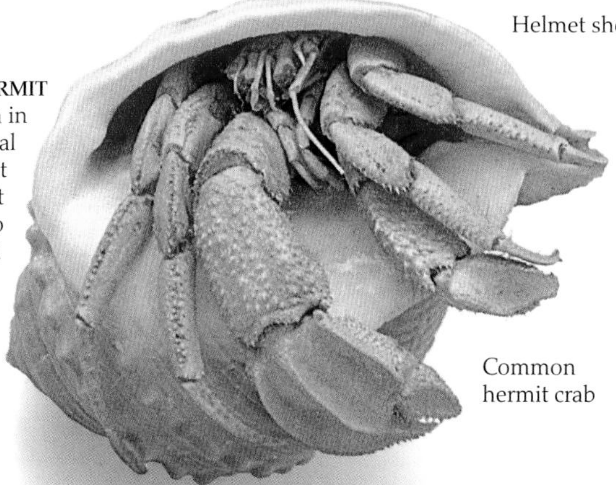

Common hermit crab

Scallop shell embedded in sponge

Roman jar

COMFORTABLE ACCOMMODATION
Some shells can even be found embedded in soft sections of natural sponge. This is often because the sponge grew over a dead shell, but sometimes a mollusk will deliberately select this soft site as its home, as in the case of the scallop shell seen here.

IS IT A BIRD... ?
Goose barnacles are crustaceans that can live, attached by a stalk, to almost any object floating in the sea—including the hulls of boats and ships. Goose barnacles are so called because of the similarity between their shells and fleshy stalks and the white head and black neck of a certain type of goose. It used to be thought that the barnacles "grew up" and turned into birds.

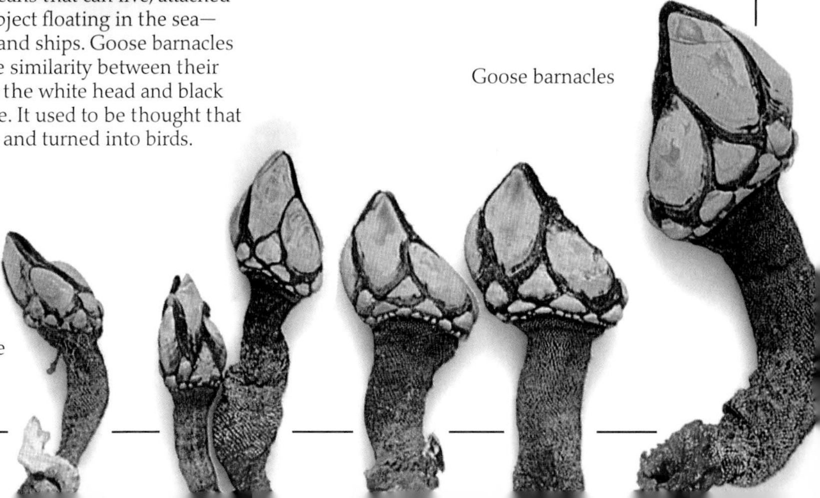

Goose barnacles

Barnacle goose

Collecting shells

SHELL COLLECTING IS A POPULAR and satisfying hobby, and a walk along the beach may be enough to start a collection. It is sometimes tempting to collect living creatures, since their shells are often in better condition than those that have been tossed around by waves or weathered by the elements. But check the local laws first—it is illegal in some places to collect live specimens. Treat everything you touch with care, and, if you are overturning rocks or coral slabs to look underneath, make sure you return them to their original position.

ON THE BEACH
Rock pools are often teeming with life, and shells that would normally be found only in deeper waters are sometimes stranded there. It pays to look closely because many creatures seek the darkness and moisture found in rock crevices or underneath stones.

COLLECTING UNDER WATER
Collecting under water reveals many shells in their natural habitats. You can use a snorkel in shallow waters, and, with proper training, scuba diving will open up a new world.

Plastic collecting bags

Mask and snorkel

TOOLS OF THE TRADE
A keen pair of eyes is the first thing needed by the collector, since living shells seldom display the bright colors seen in collections. A knife is useful for prying shells off rocks (ask an adult to help you), and some kind of collecting bag is essential. Strainers with a range of mesh sizes enable you to separate shells of different sizes quickly.

Strong penknife

Shells, rocks, and weeds separated from sand

Strainer for sorting small shells from sand

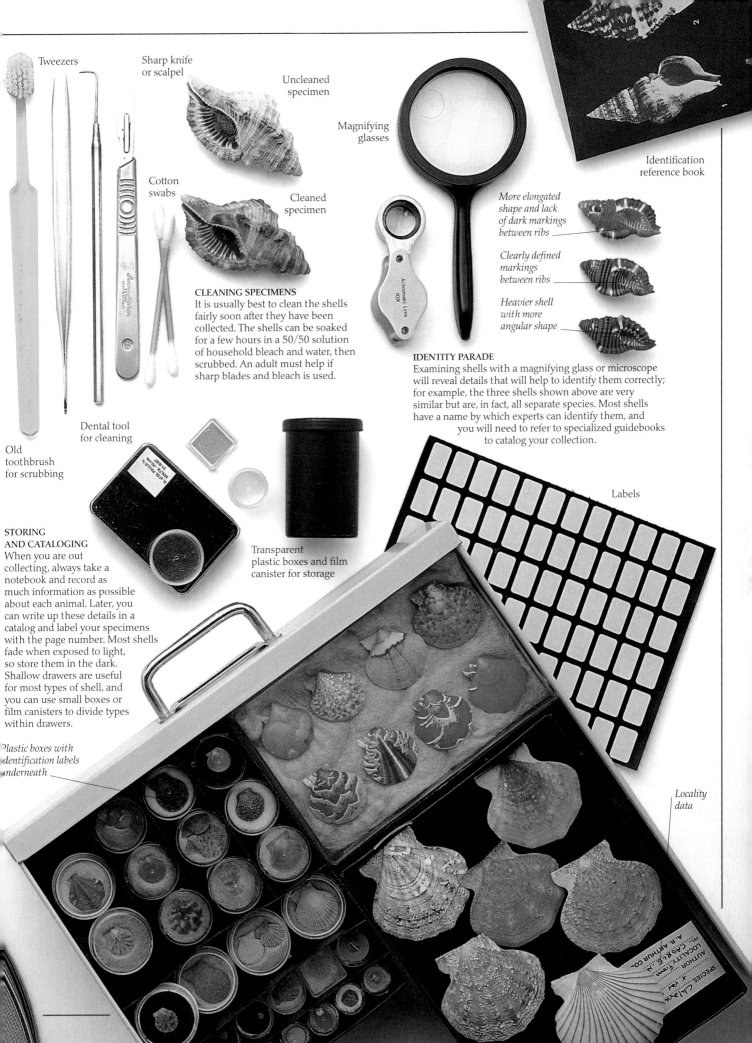

Tweezers

Sharp knife
or scalpel

Uncleaned
specimen

Magnifying
glasses

Identification
reference book

Cotton
swabs

Cleaned
specimen

*More elongated
shape and lack
of dark markings
between ribs*

*Clearly defined
markings
between ribs*

*Heavier shell
with more
angular shape*

CLEANING SPECIMENS
It is usually best to clean the shells
fairly soon after they have been
collected. The shells can be soaked
for a few hours in a 50/50 solution
of household bleach and water, then
scrubbed. An adult must help if
sharp blades and bleach is used.

IDENTITY PARADE
Examining shells with a magnifying glass or microscope
will reveal details that will help to identify them correctly;
for example, the three shells shown above are very
similar but are, in fact, all separate species. Most shells
have a name by which experts can identify them, and
you will need to refer to specialized guidebooks
to catalog your collection.

Old
toothbrush
for scrubbing

Dental tool
for cleaning

Labels

**STORING
AND CATALOGING**
When you are out
collecting, always take a
notebook and record as
much information as possible
about each animal. Later, you
can write up these details in a
catalog and label your specimens
with the page number. Most shells
fade when exposed to light,
so store them in the dark.
Shallow drawers are useful
for most types of shell, and
you can use small boxes or
film canisters to divide types
within drawers.

Transparent
plastic boxes and film
canister for storage

*Plastic boxes with
identification labels
underneath*

*Locality
data*

SPECIES C.A.J.x.m.

AUTHOR
A. R. ARTHUR CO...

LOCALITY. From
m... C.A.S.R.L.E...

Shell shapes

YOU CAN TELL A LOT ABOUT AN ANIMAL JUST BY LOOKING AT ITS SHELL.
Every group of shelled animal has a particular set of characteristics that will help
identify it. Any shell that has jointed legs or other appendages, such as pincers, is
an arthropod. The most common arthropods on land are insects and spiders; in the
ocean they are generally crustaceans, such as crabs or barnacles. However, the most
common shelled animals of all are mollusks. These have hard, curving shells that
grow around the animal's soft body. After the animal dies and the soft parts decay
away, the hard shell remains for many years. Each type of mollusk has a distinctive
shell shape and knowing a few simple rules makes them easy to identify.

Tusk shells

Scaphopods are
better known by
the name "tusk
shell," for reasons
that are clear to see.
These deep-sea
mollusks are rarely
found washed up on
beaches but are easy to
identify from their
curved, tusklike shape.
They range from just
¼ in (5 mm) long
to around 6 in (15 cm).

Tusk
shape

*Ridges
along shell*

Bivalves

This set of mollusks has shells that are in two halves—or valves—
connected by a hinge that is held together with strong muscles. Most
of the bivalve shells found on a beach have broken away from their
other half. Bivalve shells are normally
matching pairs, with each
half looking like
its partner.

Discus shape   Fan shape   Boat shape

Paddle
shape   Triangular
shape   Irregular
shape   Heart
shape

Gastropods

Three-quarters of mollusks are gastropods. Members of this group have many common names, such as snails, whelks, winkles, and limpets. They all have a single shell, often twisted into a spiral but sometimes with a smooth rounded case. Each shell has an opening, or aperture, where the animal's foot sticks out.

Aperture

Cap shape

Ear shape

Top shape

Corkscrew shape

Spindle shape

Club shape

Barrel shape

Egg shape

Irregular shape

Pear shape

Cephalopods

This group of mollusk includes the largest and most intelligent invertebrates in the world. Most of them, such as the giant squid and octopus, have no outer shell. The nautiluses, the only shelled members of this group, have shells that form in an expanding spiral.

Animal lives in largest, outermost chamber

Helmet shape

Chitons

The shells of these mollusks are made of eight separate valves that form bands of armor across the back. The valves allow the chiton to flex so it can move easily over uneven surfaces as well as roll into a ball when dislodged from the seabed.

Shield shape

Shells from the past

SHELLS ARE BUILT TO LAST—many are toughened with chemicals that make them as hard as stone. Almost all fossils are formed from hard body parts. The fossil record is evidence of animals living in the past. Sometimes these ancient animals are very similar to ones that are around today. Paleontologists, or fossil experts, use fossils to unravel the mystery of how life has changed over the years—and shells are important pieces in the puzzle.

STATELY FOSSIL, FLORIDA
The state stone of Florida is called agatized coral. It is formed from the hard outer skeletons of tiny long-dead corals that lived in the warm seas that once covered the region.

NORTH
AMERICA

SOUTH
AMERICA

FIRST CRUSTACEANS, CANADA
The Burgess Shale is a type of rock found in the Rocky Mountains of Canada. It was formed more than 500 million years ago and contains the remains of many early animals. This fossil is called *Canadaspis*. It is one of the earliest crustaceans ever found.

ORTHOCONE, NEW YORK
Early relatives of today's cephalopods were the orthocones. These were squidlike creatures that lived inside long twisted shells. Many of their fossils have been found in New York state dating back 470 million years. Some orthocones grew to nearly 30 ft (9 m) long!

GIANT TURTLE, SOUTH DAKOTA
In 1895, the shell of *Archelon*, the largest turtle ever found, was unearthed in South Dakota. The turtle lived around 70 million years ago and was almost 16½ ft (5 m) wide and 13 ft (4 m) long.

FORAMS, MEDITERRANEAN SEA
In the 1950s, a chemist named Harold Urey devised a way to take the temperature of an ancient ocean. He looked for fossils of tiny shelled creatures called forams in rocks that formed on seabeds millions of years ago. In warm water, the foram shells contain large amounts of an unusual type of oxygen.

OLD REPTILE, POLAND
In 2012, the shell of a turtle that lived 215 million years ago was found at a garbage dump in southern Poland. It is one of the oldest examples of a turtle and shows that turtles had evolved well before most dinosaurs.

DINO NEST, MONGOLIA
In the 1920s, a nest of fossilized eggs was found in Mongolia. The eggs were about 70 million years old. They did not belong to a bird or lizard, but to the dinosaur *Protoceratops*. They were the first evidence that dinosaurs laid eggs.

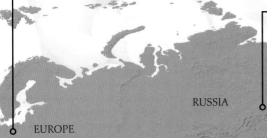

EUROPE

RUSSIA

ASIA

AFRICA

AUSTRALASIA

OLDEST HARD SHELL, NAMIBIA
In 2002, a shell-like skeleton of a coral or sponge was found among the remains of a huge reef discovered in the deserts of Namibia. This 550-million-year-old creature is the oldest known hard-shelled animal.

MYSTERIOUS FIND, AUSTRALIA
The hills of South Australia have some ancient and mysterious fossils, which may be the earliest animals ever found—dating back almost 600 million years. One of them, called *Arkarua*, looks like a tiny sand dollar. No one knows if it is a fossil shell or the remains of a completely different—and long extinct—creature.

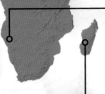

FOSSIL GEMS

Ammonites are an extinct type of mollusk. They died out around 65 million years ago, at the same time as the dinosaurs. Coiled ammonite shells are common fossils, sometimes made even more beautiful by colorful minerals.

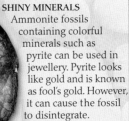

PEARLY AMMONITE
Most ammonite fossils are formed by rocky minerals filling in the spaces inside the shell, so what we see is the inside surface. In rare cases, the pearly inner shell lining is still there.

SNAKE STONE
The coiled shells of fossil ammonites once housed a squidlike mollusk living in the open end of the shell. The ridges formed walls inside the shell, creating gas-filled chambers that allowed the animal to float in water.

SHINY MINERALS
Ammonite fossils containing colorful minerals such as pyrite can be used in jewellery. Pyrite looks like gold and is known as fool's gold. However, it can cause the fossil to disintegrate.

ANCIENT EGG, MADAGASCAR
There are many stories from the Indian Ocean region of terrifying giant birds, including the Roc that attacked Sinbad the Sailor in the *Arabian Nights*. Until 1,000 years ago, huge 10-ft- (3-m-) tall elephant birds lived in Madagascar. Fossil egg shells show that they laid the biggest eggs of any bird known.

A world of shells

IT MAY NOT BE OBVIOUS AT FIRST, but shells are everywhere. They are a common sight in natural habitats and we eat many shelled animals, including lobsters and snails. But when shells have finished doing their job protecting animals living inside, people often use them for a whole range of purposes. Stone Age humans used sharp scallop shells as knives and scrapers, while in modern times, scientists are investigating how to use the shrimp shells discarded by food manufacturers to absorb uranium from seawater for use in nuclear power plants.

COPYING SHELLS

We can learn a lot from shells. A shell is both tough and lightweight, which is a very useful combination. Engineers and inventors have copied the structure of shells many times to make a range of things, from vast buildings to bulletproof vests.

Testudo
formation

DIVING SUIT
By putting on this suit a diver can become half-human, half-crustacean, with pincers instead of hands. The suit also provides a tough shell that protects the body from the huge pressures in deep water that would otherwise crush a person.

Artwork of
a Newtsuit

SHIELD DEFENSE
Roman legions beat many enemies for centuries, thanks to a range of weapons and trained soldiers. One of the tactics they used was the *testudo* (Latin for "tortoise"), where a squad of soldiers used their shields to form a shell that protected them from arrows.

CONCRETE SHELL
The Oceànografic in Valencia, Spain, is the largest aquarium in Europe. It is home to whales, dolphins, sharks, and many other sea creatures, including shelled ones, which all live under a curved dome of concrete. Like a shell, this roof is thin but strong.

Oceànografic

SHELLS IN OUR LIVES

The huge variety of shells, coming in such a wealth of colors and shapes, means they have often been used in jewelry and art. Most cultures regard certain types of shell as special, or even sacred.

IN TRADITION
During Easter, the Christian spring festival, people decorate egg shells and share chocolates in the shape of eggs. The tradition comes from the Viking idea that hares (the Easter bunny) laid eggs in fields in spring. They were actually the eggs of plovers.

Easter egg

IN MUSIC
This curious musical instrument is a traditional rattle made by Native American tribes of eastern North America. The hollow shell was filled with bone fragments or cherry stones to create a noisy shaker. Elsewhere turtle shells are also used to make simple stringed instruments, similar to guitars.

North American rattle

A devotee blowing a conch

IN RELIGION
Large conch shells (sea snails) are used by both Hindus and Buddhists to make sacred horns called *shankhas*, blown during religious rites. In Hindu tradition, the shell is an emblem of the god Vishnu.

Necklace

DRESSING UP
Tiny cowrie shells (rounded sea snails) have smooth surfaces that can be polished easily. They are among the most common shells used in jewelry and decorations.

WHO'S THE TALLEST?

Shells come in a mind-boggling array of shapes and sizes. Some are too small to see, such as the microscopic shells that form chalk and other rocks, while others are immense. The giant clam has a shell more than 3 ft (1 m) across—with enough room for a person to sit inside. Take a look at how some other record-breaking shells compare to the human body.

9 ft (2.7 m)

7 ft (2.1 m)

6 ft (1.8 m)

36 in (91 cm)

7 in (18 cm)

Ostrich egg

Syrinx aruanus (sea snail)

Leatherback turtle

Giant spider crab

Human being

Glossary

ABALONE A type of sea snail that lives on the seabed of shallow coastal waters. Many abalones are edible.

ADDUCTOR MUSCLE A large muscle used by a bivalve to pull its hinged shell shut. The muscle is so strong that it is almost impossible to pull the shell open again.

AMMONITE A cephalopod mollusk with a coiled shell that is divided into several chambers. Ammonites are extinct and were wiped out at the same time as the dinosaurs.

APERTURE A small opening; in gastropods a mouthlike opening through which the muscular foot protrudes.

APPENDAGE A term for a body part that projects from the main body; a limb, feeler, or tentacle are appendages.

AQUALUNG A breathing apparatus for divers that allows them to inhale an air mixture from a tank and then exhale through a valve into the water.

ARTHROPODS The largest group of animals alive today; it includes insects, spiders, and crustaceans. The name arthropod means jointed foot, and refers to the fact that all members of this group have legs made up of several jointed sections.

BARNACLE A crustacean that spends most of its life glued to a rock. It does not walk on its legs, but instead sweeps them through water to sift particles of food.

BIVALVE A type of mollusk that has a shell in two halves that are connected by a hinge.

BRACHIOPOD A sea animal with a shell split in two, top to bottom, and hinged at the back.

BUOYANCY CHAMBER A gas-filled section inside certain mollusk shells, especially the nautilus, which helps the animal float.

BYSSAL THREADS (BYSSUS) The tough, hairlike threads that mussels use to secure themselves to rocks or other hard surfaces.

CALCIUM CARBONATE A chemical made from calcium, carbon, and oxygen. It makes shells hard and rigid.

Common spider conch shell
(*Lambis lambis*)

Lobster, an arthropod

CAMOUFLAGE Patterns on the surface of a shell, or any other body part, that allow an animal to blend in with its surroundings, making it harder for predators to spot the creature.

CARAPACE A general term for a shell that covers a body; specifically referring to the upper shell of a tortoise or turtle. The lower shell is called the plastron.

CEPHALOPOD A group of mollusk that has largely lost its shells. Cephalopods include octopuses, squids, and cuttlefish.

CHELONIA The scientific name for the order of reptiles that includes tortoises, turtles, and terrapins.

CHITIN A flexible material made of sugars. Arthropods such as insects and crustaceans use chitin to make their stiff exoskeleton.

COCKSCOMB A type of mussel that lives in freshwater and produces some of the best pearls.

COLUMELLA The central, spiral part of the shell of certain gastropods (snails). It is shaped like a spiral staircase.

CONCH A large sea snail. Conch shells can be used to make a loud horn or trumpet.

CONCHIOLIN The complex scaffold of proteins and other chemicals that forms the shape of a mollusk's shell and is then strengthened with calcium carbonate.

COPEPODS A group of tiny crustaceans, which float in water in huge numbers. Some copepods are known as fish lice.

CRUSTACEANS A large group of arthropods that includes crabs, lobsters, krill, and barnacles. Most of them live in water but a few types, such as woodlice, live on land, although normally in damp areas.

CUTTLEBONE A soft shell shaped like a surfboard that is often found washed up on the beach. This is the internal shell of a cuttlefish, a cephalopod mollusk that lives near the seafloor.

DECAPODS A large group of crustaceans that have 10 legs. Decapods include crabs, lobsters, crayfish, and shrimp.

DETRITUS The waste produced by life including droppings and the remains of dead animals and plants.

ECHINODERM A group of animals with shell-like plates of calcium carbonate under their skin. Echinoderms include sea urchins, sea lilies, and starfish.

ENDANGERED In danger—endangered life forms are those that may become extinct unless people act to protect them.

ESTUARY A wide river mouth where salty sea water mixes with fresh river water as the tides flood in and out.

EXHALANT SIPHON A nozzle through which mollusks can pump a current of water to help them move. It also helps in respiration, feeding, and breeding.

EXOSKELETON A hard outer covering of an animal, especially an arthropod. The exoskeleton gives the body its shape.

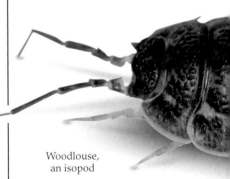

Woodlouse, an isopod

FILTER FEEDER An animal that survives by sifting food items from water.

GASTROPODS A large group of mollusk, including slugs, most of which have one shell around their bodies and which move around on a single muscular foot. These animals live in the ocean, freshwater, and on land. They are more often referred to as snails.

GIRDLE A structure that encircles the shells of chitons, a type of mollusk. In general, a girdle is a large and tight belt that holds the shell plates together.

HABITAT The place where animals and plants live. Every habitat has some resources to help sustain life and some challenges for animals to overcome for their survival.

HIBERNATION An inactive, sleeplike state used by many animals to save energy in winter. They stop eating and their body processes slow down.

HINGE The flexible connection between the two valves, or shells, of a bivalve or brachiopod, that allows the shells to open and close.

INHALANT SIPHON A nozzle used to suck water into the shell so that a mollusk can filter food from it.

INVERTEBRATE An animal that lacks a backbone. In other words, anything that is not a vertebrate.

Sundial shell, a gastropod

ISOPOD A type of crustacean with a flexible shell made from several plates.

KERATIN Protein material that forms the outer covering of turtle and tortoise shells and forms horn sheaths, fingernails, and claws, and the hair of vertebrates.

LIGAMENTS A tough connective tissue found in bivalves that joins the two halves of the shell together at the hinge (and also connects bones in other animals).

LIMPETS Cone-shaped relatives of snails that live on rocky seashores. When under water, they graze on seaweed, but as the tide goes out the limpets return to a spot on the rock and pull their shell down to the surface to prevent them from drying out in the air.

MANTLE This secretes chemicals, to make a shell, as well as enclosing the mantle cavity, which contains many of the body organs of a mollusk. A similar structure is seen in brachiopods.

MICROSCOPIC Describes something so small that it cannot be seen without a magnifying glass or microscope.

MIGRATORY Referring to an animal that migrates or makes a regular journey each year to find better places to spend the winter, or avoid difficult conditions, or to breed.

MOLLUSK A member of a very large group of shelled animal including snails, clams, and octopuses.

MOLT To shed the skin or exoskeleton.

NACRE Also known as mother of pearl, this rainbow-colored shiny material forms the inner lining of mollusk shells. It forms the layers of a pearl.

NATURALIST Someone interested in nature and wildlife.

NAUTILUS A relative of the octopus and squid that has a full shell.

NUMMULITE A nearly extinct foram; a minute creature with a shell that has pores through which it feeds. Most nummulites are found as fossils.

OMNIVORE An animal that eats both animal and plant food.

OPERCULUM A lidlike flap that stops a snail from drying out. It is drawn over the shell's opening when the animal withdraws into its shell.

PLANKTON Organisms that float or swim in water and have no control over where the current takes them.

PLASTRON The lower shell of a turtle.

POLYP The soft body of a coral that is surrounded by a calcium carbonate skeleton.

SANDBAR (OR SANDBANK) A sandy area on a shallow seabed that is often exposed to the air by the falling tide.

SCAPHOPODS A class of mollusk better known as tusk shells because their shells look like the tusk of an elephant. These animals live in the soft seabed far from land.

SINISTRAL Referring to a shell that twists to the left. Most shells are dextral, meaning they twist to the right.

SIPHONS The tubes that mollusks use to take in and expel water.

TELSON The rear segment of a crustacean, often referred to as the "tail."

TEST Another word for a shell or hard body structure. Sea urchins have tests, as do microscopic forams and diatoms. Diatoms have tests made from silica, the same chemical compound as in sand.

TRITON The ancient Greek god of the sea. A type of snail shell is named triton in his honor.

TYRIAN This refers to the ancient city of Tyre on the eastern coast of the Mediterranean Sea in what is now Lebanon. This region was a large producer of Tyrian purple dye made from the shells of certain sea snails.

UNIVALVE A mollusk with a single shell covering its body.

URCHIN A spiny echinoderm that scrapes algae from rocks under water. A sea urchin normally has a rounded body, divided into five segments.

VALVE The term used for a section of shell. Univalve creatures have one shell section, while bivalves have two.

VELIGER The young form of a sea snail that is small enough to float in the water as plankton.

VERTEBRATE An animal with a backbone made from many interlinking sections called vertebrae. Vertebrates

Sea urchin

include fish, frogs, lizards, birds, and mammals. The only truly shelled vertebrates are turtles and tortoises.

VOLUTE A type of sea snail that hunts prey on the seabed. Most have very ornate shells.

VIVIPAROUS Describes an animal that gives birth to its young instead of laying eggs.

WHORL The name given to one complete turn of a mollusk shell. Most large snail shells, for example, have several whorls.

Index

Acknowledgments

Dorling Kindersley would like to thank:
David Attard (Malta), Andrew Clarke (British Antarctic Survey); Derek Coombes; Geoff Cox, Koën Fraussen (Belgium); Dr. Ray Ingle, Dr. Roger Lincoln, Colin McCarthy, Chris Owen, and Andrew Stimson of the British Museum (Natural History); Samuel Jones (Pearls) Ltd.; Sue Mennell; Alistair Moncur; José Maria Hernandez Otero (Spain); Tom and Celia Pain; Respectable Reptiles; Alan Seccombe; Dr. Francisco Garcia Talavera, Museum of Santa Cruz (Natural History); Ken Wye (Eaton's Shell Shop); John Youles.
Helen Peters for the index
Monica Byles for proofreading
Rob Houston for editorial assistance
Mike Pilley and Fred Ford of Radius Graphics
Karl Shone for special photography on pages 6–7 and 40–41
Jane Burton for special photography on page 59

Picture credits
(t=top, b=bottom, c=center, l=left, r=right)
Alamy Images: Steve Trewhella 49cla, WaterFrame 71c; Corbis: Ingo Arndt / Minden Pictures 39clb, Clouds Hill Imaging Ltd. 24tl, Jason Edwards / National Geographic Society 66bl, The Gallery Collection 69tr, Julian Kumar / Godong 69cr, Massimo Listri 10tl, Pete Oxford / Minden Pictures 31bl, Jeffrey L. Rotman 45tc, D. Sheldon / F1 Online 61bl, Wim van Egmond / Visuals Unlimited 66br, Visuals Unlimited 57bl, 66tr, David Wrobel / Visuals Unlimited 52bl; Dorling Kindersley: The American Museum of Natural History 69ca, Natural History Museum, London 38bl, 67tr, 67clb, 67crb, Wallace Collection, London 22br, Jerry Young 7tr; Doug Allan: 26; Dreamstime.com: Dvest 26tl (background), 66-67 (Background), 68-69 (Background), 70-71 (Background), Regien Paassen 68cl, Pkruger 71crb, Pzaxe 70-71bc;

The Ancient Art & Architecture Collection: 44br
Getty Images: Allan Baxter / The Image Bank 68b, Robyn Beck / AFP 67br, Grant Faint / Photographer's Choice 11tc, Michel Gangne / AFP 34cr, mark hughes / Flickr 34bl, Joel Sartore / National Geographic 56cr, Science & Society Picture Library 69cl, Janek Skarzynski / AFP 67tl; Heather Angel: 20, 25, 40tl & cr, 46tr, 54tl Ardea London: 29tr, 35cr
Axel Poignant Archive: 39MR
BBC Hulton Picture Library: 37t&bl
The Bridgeman Art Library/Uffizi Gallery, Florence: 16
The Bridgeman Art Library/Alan Jacobs Gallery, London: 22tr
Bruce Coleman Ltd.: 7tr
Mary Evans Picture Library: 8, 11, 12, 15, 19br, 22br, 26tl, 28tl, 30tr, 34tl & cr, 36br, 50tl, 57 tl & cr, 59cr
The Kobal Collection/20th-Century Fox: 14

National Museum of Wales: 38bl
Planet Earth Pictures/Seaphot: 19cl, 24br, 27, 42, 52tl, 53tc& bc, 58bl
Science Photo Library: Alan Sirulnikoff 66cl, Sheila Terry 66c, Paul Wootton 68tr
Rothschild Estate: 30br
Robert Harding Picture Library: 55bl 54, 56, 58

Jacket images: *Front:* Corbis: Radius Images b

Wallchart: Corbis: clb; Dreamstime.com: Brad Calkins crb/ (Yellow Snail)

Illustrators: Will Giles, Sandra Pond: 21b; 35t; 43b

All other images © Dorling Kindersley
For further information see:
www.dkimages.com